THE NEVADA DESERT

By

SESSIONS S. WHEELER

ILLUSTRATED WITH PHOTOGRAPHS

The CAXTON PRINTERS, Ltd.
CALDWELL, IDAHO
1972

First printing August 1971
Second printing February 1972

International Standard Book Number 0-87004-205-X
Library of Congress Catalog Card No. 72-123581

Printed and bound in the United States of America
The CAXTON PRINTERS, Ltd.
Caldwell, Idaho 83605
118053

To Lythia and To Gaylene

Preface

MICROFILM copies of the early newspapers, old journals, letters to the Commissioner of Indian Affairs, military reports, scarce books, and the memories of living persons contain exciting but not an easily obtainable history of the Nevada desert. The intent of this book is to record a small portion of this information in a form which will make it more readily available to people who enjoy the desert and western Americana.

The reader will find a number of direct quotations, especially from newspapers and journals. There were several reasons for not paraphrasing them, including the doubt that I could write them as dramatically as have W. J. Forbes, editor of the 1866 Humboldt newspaper, John C. Frémont, and others.

I wish to express gratitude to the persons—their names are mentioned in the text—who granted the hours of interviews which allowed the writing of the story of John G. Taylor and the chapter, "Memories of the Desert's Gold Seekers." The story of "desert justice" was told to me by an old Nevadan several years before his long and full life ended; and because it was so unusual, I wrote it down and filed it away—believing that someday there would be a place for it.

The job of searching the microfilm files of the old newspapers is enjoyable but time-consuming, and I wish to thank Inez Johnson, Nevada Wheeler, and Virginia Phillips for their aid when the schedule became tight.

Other good friends were of much help. Marilyn Taber and Gaylene Henderson volunteered their typing services; Jack Horgan and Victor Goodwin provided competent advice on the early trails; and Don Tuohy of the Nevada State Museum aided, as he has before, by checking the accuracy of the archeological material.

Much of the research for the book was done in the Summerfield Special Collections room of the University of Nevada Library, and I wish to thank all of its personnel for their help. I also appreciate the considerate aid extended by John Barr Tompkins during the days that I worked at the Bancroft Library. I am grateful to the Yale University Press and to the University Microfilms for permission to quote parts of several journals.

For the use of their photographs, I wish to thank the Nevada State Museum, the State of Nevada Department of Highways, the Nevada Historical Society, the Nevada Division of Parks, the National Park Service, Mrs. Mary Sebbas, Walter Mulcahy, Adrian Atwater, Jim Calhoun, Dave Basso, Thomas C. Wilson, Inez Johnson, and Clarence L. Young.

Other persons who aided in various ways and to whom I am grateful include: Phyllis Locke, Dr. William A. O'Brien, Kenneth Carpenter, Robert Armstrong, Marion Welliver, Eslie Cann, Jim Bidart, Earl W. Kersten, Margaret Wheat, Elaine Pommerening, Paul Gemmil, Alene DeRuff, Ted Laurie, Harold Curran, Clayton Phillips, Don Clendenon, Harlan Johnson, Nicholas Cady, and Dr. Effie Mona Mack.

The competence of the personnel of the University of Nevada Audio-Visual Communications Department is appreciated, and I wish to especially mention Dirck Henderson and Dave Nichols for their processing of photographs, Carole Olsen for her art work on the endsheet map, and the cooperation of Jamie Arjona and Linda Loeffler.

And finally, as always, my thanks to Margaret Pead of Caxton.

Table of Contents

Chapter   *Page*

1. THE DESERT - - - - - - - - - - - -   17

2. THE DREADED FORTY-MILE DESERT - - - - -   30

3. THE BLACK ROCK DESERT—INDIAN STRONGHOLD -   57

4. THE MOHAVE DESERT - - - - - - - - -   93

5. MEMORIES OF THE DESERT'S GOLD SEEKERS - -   107

6. DESERT GRASS AND THE BIG SPREAD - - - - -   121

7. SANCTUARY - - - - - - - - - - - - -   149

    APPENDIX A - - - - - - - - - - -   161

    APPENDIX B - - - - - - - - - - - -   163

List of Illustrations

An Old Tree Fights for Survival in the Drifting Sand
of the Forty-Mile Desert - - - - - - - - - *Frontispiece*

Page

It Was a Land Which Had Been Torn Apart and Rebuilt - - - 18

Light, Reflecting from the Surface of the Playa, Gives the
Black Rock Desert the Appearance of a Large Lake - - - - 20

Modern Covered Wagons on the Desert - - - - - - - - 22

Abandoned Houses Tell Where People Attempted To Farm - - 22

Many of the Desert's Mountain Ranges Rise More Than
Ten Thousand Feet - - - - - - - - - - - - - - - 23

A Nevada State Museum Life-Size Diorama Depicts Indian Life 25

The Arrow Maker and His Student - - - - - - - - - 26

Plant Seeds Were a Staple Food of Nevada Indians - - - - 27

The Projectiles of Two Generations Lie Close Together - - - 29

The Forty-Mile Desert's Humboldt Sink at Left of
Center Mountain, Carson Sink at Right - - - - - - - 31

The Trail Skirted Both Sides of Humboldt Lake - - - - - 31

An Oxshoe on the Trail - - - - - - - - - - - - - 33

Brady's Hot Springs on the Truckee Branch - - - - - - 33

After Crossing the Forty-Mile, Emigrants Rested at the
Big Bend of the Truckee - - - - - - - - - - - - - 35

Emigrant Graveyard at Wadsworth - - - - - - - - - 35

A Windstorm on the Forty-Mile Desert - - - - - - - - 37

Emigrants Who Started Late Faced the Hazard of
Early Winter Storms - - - - - - - - - - - - - - 43

The Remnants of a Wagon Rim on the Trail - - - - - - 50

These Hummocks Slowed the Pace of Wagons - - - - - 51

A Marker along U.S. Highway 50 at Ragtown - - - - - 53

A Few Pieces of Rusty Iron and Some Wood Still Mark
the Forty-Mile Desert Trail - - - - - - - - - - - 53

The Great Playa Appears Almost Endless in Length - - - 57

The Black Rock Desert Derived Its Name from the Mountain - 57

The Lassen Trail Traveled between the Towering Walls of
High Rock Canyon - - - - - - - - - - - - - - - 59

                                                          Page
Some Early Travelers Took Time To Record Names and Dates
    on the Cliffs of High Rock Canyon - - - - - - - - - 59
Victims of an Indian Raid on a Wagon Train Are Believed
    Buried in This Multiple Grave near the Lassen Trail - - - 61
A Section of the Trail between Lassen Meadows and Rabbithole   61
Remnant of a Sheepherder's Outfit - - - - - - - - - - 63
The Mountains Bordering the Black Rock Desert Provided
    Strongholds for Indian War Parties - - - - - - - - 63
The Currently Dry Winnemucca Lake Was Called Mud
    Lake in 1865 - - - - - - - - - - - - - - - - - 64
Fort Churchill, on the Carson River, Established in 1860 - - - 65
The Remains of the Granite Creek Station Five Miles
    North of Gerlach - - - - - - - - - - - - - - - - 72
The Indians Fired at the Men in the Granite Creek Station
    from Behind the Walls of This Corral - - - - - - - 73
Paradise Valley about the Turn of the Century - - - - - 75
Unionville's Wells Fargo Building in 1885 - - - - - - - - 75
Photograph of Fort McDermit Taken in 1887 - - - - - - 78
Colonel Charles McDermit and His Family - - - - - - - 79
Fourteen-Horse and Mule-Team Wagons Carrying Freight - - 81
Today, Little Remains of Dun Glen - - - - - - - - - 81
Part of the Long Barn of This Ranch Was One of the
    Fort Winfield Scott Buildings - - - - - - - - - - 83
Looking South from Leonard Creek - - - - - - - - - 86
Great, Jagged Mountains of Banded Limestone Rise High
    above Desert Valleys - - - - - - - - - - - - - - 95
The Mohave Desert Is the Home of the Joshua Tree - - - 95
A Bulldozer Cuts a Trench along the Tule Springs Wash - - - 96
The Sheer Walls of the Trench Allow Study of Thousands of
    Years of Deposits - - - - - - - - - - - - - - - 96
Scientists Excavate a Pile of Bison and Camel Bones - - - - 97
The Most Abundant Animal Bones Were Those of an Extinct
    Species of the Camel Family - - - - - - - - - - - 97
Pueblo Grande de Nevada at Sunrise - - - - - - - - - 99
Room Outlines of Lost City Surface Dwellings - - - - - 99
An Interesting, If Inaccurate, 1886 Map of the Desert's
    Mineral Wealth - - - - - - - - - - - - - - - - 109
Some of Rhyolite's Old Stone Walls Still Stand - - - - - 111
Goldfield in 1903, When Claude Lund First Arrived There - - 111
During Tonopah's Early Days, Its Residents Depended on
    These Wagons for Their Water - - - - - - - - - - 115
Goldfield When It Was Nevada's Largest City - - - - - - 115
The Giant Quartz Outcrop of the Getchell Mine - - - - - 119

Page

The Getchell Mine When It Was One of the Nation's
Large Producers of Gold and Tungsten - - - - - - - - 119
The Miller and Lux Quinn River Crossing Ranch in 1898 - - 123
John G. Taylor - - - - - - - - - - - - - - - - - 125
Lovelock, Nevada, in 1920 - - - - - - - - - - - - - 129
Jeanette and Her Horse at Lovelock Ranch - - - - - - 131
"John G." Preparing a Camp Lunch for Mary McCullough
and Carmen - - - - - - - - - - - - - - - - - - 133
John G. Taylor's Sheep Were Noted for Their Fine Wool - - 143
The Valley of Fire State Park in Clark County - - - - - 150
Cathedral Gorge State Park in Lincoln County - - - - - 150
The Ichthyosaur State Monument, Twenty-Three Miles
East of Gabbs - - - - - - - - - - - - - - - - - 151
The Ward Charcoal Ovens Historic State Monument - - - - 151
The Mormon Station Historic State Monument at Genoa - - - 152
The Kershaw-Ryan State Recreation Area - - - - - - - 152
The Eagle Valley State Recreation Area - - - - - - - - 153
The Beaver Dam State Park in Lincoln County - - - - - 153
Fort Churchill Historic State Monument - - - - - - - 154
Organized by Cedarville, California, People, Emigrant
Trail Buffs Followed the Lassen-Applegate Trail - - - 155
In Case of Engine Failure, a Trail Bike of Some Type
Adds a Safety Factor - - - - - - - - - - - - - 155
Old Conveyor Belts Are Used To Cross the Bottomless Mud
of a Spring Runoff - - - - - - - - - - - - - - 157
In Case the Conveyor Belt Experiment Is a Failure, There
Will Still Be Two Cars on Solid Ground - - - - - - 157
Equipment To Make a Comfortable Camp Adds to the
Enjoyment of a Desert Trip - - - - - - - - - - - 159
The High Desert's Hillsides Shine with the Silvery Gray
of Its Sagebrush - - - - - - - - - - - - - - - 159

THE NEVADA DESERT

CHAPTER I

The Desert

A S LATE AS the end of the first quarter of the nineteenth
century it was still a land of mystery—uncharted, unexplored. With the exception of the Arctic, it was a part of the
only large area of the North American continent which the
white man had not penetrated. It had remained a blank space
on the map—a challenge to men of adventure.

Its future was shaped millions of years before when great
blocks of the earth's surface tilted upwards to form the Sierra
Nevada, giant granite barriers to the west which forced storm
clouds moving inland from the Pacific to rise and cool. And
as the clouds cooled, the moisture they carried was squeezed
from them so that often little remained to dampen the region beyond.

It was a land which had been torn apart and rebuilt many
times since the earth was born. Above the sun-parched valleys, jagged mountain ranges towered solemn and massive,
their sheer walls of granite and basalt telling of the violence of
the past's awesome earthquakes and thundering volcanoes.
Rugged canyons, cut sharp and deep into native rock, testified
to erosion by silt-laden waters through the millenniums.

It had not always been an arid country. During the past
sixty thousand years, while the last great ice sheet from the
North crept down and then retreated from what is now north-
central and northeastern United States, small glaciers had
formed in the Sierras and large lakes had filled many of the
valleys. There had been long periods of ample moisture when
grasses covered the floors of southern basins, and evergreen
forests shaded vast areas to the north. Such an environment
encouraged abundant life, so that lakes and streams teemed
with fish, waterfowl thrived in the marshlands, and giant

mammoths, early types of horses, and even relatives of the camel grazed the meadows.

And there is evidence that, more than twelve thousand years before the present, man occupied the region. No one knows with certainty when the first humans arrived or how long they stayed, but it is believed they may have been far-ranging hunters whose ancestors had crossed the Bering Strait from Asia to the New World. It is thought that if and when they moved on, they were eventually replaced by other cultures of their people.

Fluctuations in the weather continued, but gradually the climate became generally warmer and drier—and eventually the land was arid again. Where lakes had sparkled for endless miles, only sand and baked mud flats remained. The great southern meadows were gone and with them the large mammals they had sustained. Clouds of white dust swept upward from alkali-coated playas as winds built dunes of shifting sand; and under the glare of the summer sun, distance had no ending.

And so, to the first white men who ventured there, the uncharted land seemed barren and forbidding—and they named it desert.

*   *   *

In the temperate zones of the North American continent, a desert is usually defined as a region of hot daytime summer temperatures, higher than average evaporation rates, and—most important—less than ten inches of precipitation annually. In amounts of rain and snow falling on its rugged surface, Nevada is the driest—and has the largest percentage of its total area classified as desert—of all states in the Union.

Contributing to its uniqueness, nature divided it into two main desert regions. Most of the northern two-thirds of the state is included within the largest of the North American deserts, the Great Basin Desert[1] which is often called Nevada's "high" or "cool" desert. The southern one-third of the state,

_____

1. Jaeger, Edmund C., *The North American Deserts* (Stanford, Calif.: Stanford University Press, 1957).

Courtesy Adrian Atwater
IT WAS A LAND WHICH HAD BEEN
TORN APART AND REBUILT MANY
TIMES.

where valley floors have lower elevations, is a portion of the Mohave Desert[2]—the "low" or "warm" desert.

Each area has its distinctive beauty. During early mornings and evenings, the high desert's upland valleys[3] and hillsides shine with the silvery gray of its dominant shrubs, the sagebrush and shad scale; and after a summer thunderstorm, the pleasant odor of sagebrush saturates the air. The Mohave, with its widely spaced creosote bushes, odd Joshua trees, and gray desert soil is probably more spectacular—the type of desert usually portrayed in motion pictures.

Except for the state's southern tip where drainage flows to the Colorado River, and its northeastern extreme where river waters eventually reach the Columbia, Nevada lies within the Great Basin—a land of interior drainage where streams lose their identity in lakes and marshes or beneath the ground instead of contributing their waters to the sea. Along the perimeters of the high desert's valleys, mountain canyons contain springs or small streams. Many of the streams flow only short distances beyond their canyon mouths before sinking from sight into valley floors; but others, fed by the rain and snow falling on larger high-elevation areas, provide irrigation water for the state's ranches. Originating from extensive watersheds in the Sierra Nevadas, the Truckee and Walker rivers flow eastward to desert lakes, and the Carson makes its way to its sink northeast of Fallon. The Humboldt is the state's longest river, originating in the mountains of northeastern Nevada and flowing westward through the high desert approximately three hundred miles to where its sink adjoins that of the Carson River. Because of its meandering, it is estimated that its water actually flows almost a thousand miles. People from less arid states are often amazed at the small size of some of the Nevada streams which official maps title rivers.

Mountain ranges, many of which rise more than ten thousand feet above sea level, extend their lengths in a general

---

2. Mohave is also spelled "Mojave."
3. Some geographers classify the higher and wetter areas of the Great Basin Desert as steppe or semidesert. These areas generally receive from seven to ten inches of precipitation, and their dominant plant is the sagebrush.

LIGHT, REFLECTING FROM THE SURFACE OF THE PLAYA, GIVES THE BLACK ROCK DESERT THE APPEARANCE OF THE LARGE LAKE IT ONCE WAS THOUSANDS OF YEARS AGO.

Modern Covered Wagons on the Desert

Abandoned Houses Tell Where People Attempted To Farm Where There Was
Too Little Water.

north-south direction and divide the state into a series of flat-floored valleys. In the high desert many of these valleys and their surrounding upland areas provide grazing for cattle and sheep; while others, once covered by prehistoric lakes or marshes, are flats of baked mud coated with alkali salts in which only specially adapted plants can survive. Early emigrants and settlers considered several of these playas as individual deserts and named them as such.

To some who hurry along Nevada highways, the country through which they pass seems almost barren of life. But to those who know it, the desert is the home of a myriad of living things—animals and plants capable of solving their problems of survival in intensely interesting ways.

The desert's mountain ranges provide climatic and biologic islands where juniper and piñon pines form the most widespread forests. Other species of conifers grow in limited areas, and shrubs and deciduous trees along streams and around springs offer shade and food to game mammals and birds.

MANY OF THE DESERT'S MOUNTAIN RANGES RISE MORE THAN TEN THOUSAND FEET ABOVE SEA LEVEL.

The mountains of the southern desert have the largest number of Nelson desert bighorn sheep found in North America, and mule deer range over most of the state. Other large mammals include the pronghorn antelope and the interesting carnivores—the coyote, cougar, and bobcat. Sage grouse, chukar partridge, and other game birds and small game mammals exist in areas where the habitat is suitable for their needs; and several of the desert's sinks receive enough drainage water to form marshes which attract thousands of migratory waterfowl each year. Most of the lakes, rivers, and even the smaller streams contain trout and other fish, and of special interest to the naturalists are several endemic species such as the cui-ui of Pyramid Lake and certain minnows found in desert springs.

But in the most barren appearing areas are creatures which, in some ways, are the most interesting of all. Small mammals, such as the kangaroo rat, are largely nocturnal—carrying on most of their life processes at night, when the desert is cool. Underground-dwelling amphibians race through their complex life history of egg, tadpole, and adult before a thunderstorm's pool of water dries, and beautifully colored and distinctively marked lizards appear as miniatures of the great prehistoric reptiles. Various species of snakes, unusual birds, the desert tortoise, and odd insects make the desert a fascinating showcase of specialized animals ingeniously adapted to an arid land.

In the desert plants nature's unique devices for survival are also noticeable. Leaves are coated or specially constructed to minimize loss of water, and roots delve deep into the earth to reach underground water tables or form widely spreading, near-surface networks so as to absorb every possible drop of rain. Seeds, which remain dormant during years of insufficient moisture, quickly germinate after ample spring rains and grow rapidly to maturity so as to produce a new generation of their species before soils dry. Their flowers of brilliant colors bring the desert dazzling beauty.

At the time of the white man's arrival, four main groups of Indians lived within the boundaries of the Nevada desert.

A NEVADA STATE MUSEUM LIFE-SIZE DIORAMA DEPICTS INDIAN LIFE BEFORE THE
WHITE MAN CAME TO NEVADA.

Courtesy Nevada State Museum
THE ARROW MAKER AND HIS STUDENT

The Southern Paiutes occupied areas of the far south; the Shoshoni Indians were spread over east-central Nevada; the Northern Paiutes covered most of the northwestern half of the state; and the Washoe Indians were confined to a relatively small area around Lake Tahoe and the eastern base of the Sierras.

All the desert dwellers were seminomadic hunters and gatherers, although it is believed that the Southern Paiutes did irrigate and grow corn, beans, squash, and sunflowers on a few small plots in the vicinity of streams. Both the Southern Paiute and Shoshoni made pottery for cooking purposes which was unadorned with the paint and decorations characteristic of the pottery of Pueblo cultures.

Courtesy Nevada State Museum

PLANT SEEDS WERE A STAPLE FOOD OF NEVADA INDIANS

The Northern Paiutes apparently controlled the abundant fisheries of northwestern Nevada's large Pyramid and Walker lakes, as well as the marshes of the Humboldt and Carson sinks. The native fish of the lakes and the edible plants and waterfowl of the marshes provided an important resource for these people.

While the languages of the Southern and Northern Paiutes and the Shoshoni showed a relationship, the language of the Washoe Indians was of a different stock—related to that of Indians in California, Mexico, and Central America. Beautiful baskets made by Washoe Indian women are valued by collectors throughout the nation.

Although in 1776 the great Franciscan explorer, Father Garces, visited a Mohave Indian village across the Colorado River from Nevada's southern tip, most historians believe that Jedediah Strong Smith and his party of Rocky Mountain Fur Company trappers were the first white explorers to cross the Nevada desert. Setting out from the Great Salt Lake in the summer of 1826, Smith and his men traveled southwesterly, moving across a section of southern Nevada before eventually reaching the Mission San Gabriel in California. In late May of 1827, hoping to find a more direct route for the return trip, Smith and two of his men made their way over the Sierras, probably by way of Ebbets Pass, and struck out through the central part of the desert.

It was a fearsome journey with thirst, hunger, deep sand, and unbearable heat constantly threatening tragedy. But in early July they reached their headquarters camp. They had challenged the mysterious land and they had survived.

Others soon followed. During the next two years the Hudson's Bay Company's Peter Skene Ogden explored the three-hundred-mile length of the Humboldt River; and in 1833 Joseph Walker blazed additions to Ogden's Humboldt route and established a trail which, in a few years, thousands of California-bound emigrants would travel. The first of these, the Bartleson-Bidwell party, crossed the desert in 1841.

During 1843 and '44, John Charles Frémont, searching for the legendary San Buenaventura River which was believed to

THE PROJECTILES OF TWO GENERATIONS LIE CLOSE TOGETHER ON A
NAVY TARGET RANGE.

flow from the Utah mountains to San Francisco Bay, explored
northwestern and southern Nevada, discovered beautiful Pyramid Lake, and wrote a journal of his travels.

Soon thousands of oxen, mules, horses, and humans were
struggling across the Nevada desert en route to California and
Oregon. A few stopped and settled along the way, and eventually others returned to share the harvest of the desert's wealth.

It was no longer an uncharted, unexplored land.

CHAPTER II

The Dreaded Forty-Mile Desert

TO EARLY EMIGRANTS, the Forty-mile Desert was not far short of Hades.

At St. Joseph, Council Bluffs, Independence, and other border towns where their great western journey began, they listened to the stories of the dangers they faced in crossing this small portion of the Great Basin; and as they traveled toward it for more than seventeen hundred miles, rumors were passed back along the trail which increased their apprehensions.

The so-called Forty-mile Desert trail began southwest of Big Meadows (Lovelock Valley), skirted the Humboldt Lake, and branched into two entirely different routes to California.

The right-hand fork, which led to the Big Bend of the Truckee River (Wadsworth), traveled over rocky foothills and deep sand areas—and offered one source of water (Brady's Hot Springs) along its length. The other route, which turned to the south to skirt the edge of the playa of the Carson Sink, intersected the Carson River at a place which became known as Ragtown. Both trails were of about the same length, and neither offered enough grass or browse to sustain the draft animals.

Driving today at a mile or more a minute over Interstate Highway 80, which largely parallels, on its south side, the trail to the Truckee River—or along U.S. Highway 95, which in some places is only yards to the east of the old tracks of the Carson route—it may seem difficult to believe that this sunny, pleasant country was once the most feared section of the entire California trail. But the diaries of some of the 1849 travelers, especially the journal written by Mrs. Sarah Royce, provide an understanding.

Mrs. Royce, her husband, and their two-year-old daughter,

Courtesy Walter Mulcahy

THE FORTY-MILE DESERT'S HUMBOLDT SINK (AT THE LEFT OF CENTER MOUNTAIN) ADJOINS THE CARSON SINK AT THE RIGHT.

THE TRAIL SKIRTED BOTH SIDES OF HUMBOLDT LAKE. THIS ROAD MARKS ITS LOCATION ON THE EAST SIDE.

Mary, did not leave Council Bluffs until June 10—more than a month after approximately twenty-two thousand humans[1] and possibly sixty thousand livestock had started along the trail. The necessity for crossing the Sierra Nevadas before snow closed the passes into California made a late start especially dangerous, and the difficulty of finding grass for draft animals along a corridor through which thousands of other livestock had passed was an additional handicap.

After considerable hardship, the Royces were within two days' travel to the headwaters of the Humboldt (Mary's) River on about September 14. The section of Mrs. Royce's book,[2] which provides a remarkable account of a desperate journey across the Forty-mile Desert, begins there.

". . . we met a band of Mormons who had been gold hunting in California for the summer, and were on their return to Salt Lake. This was the company whose leader was to tell us how we might get from the Sink of the Humboldt, otherwise Mary's River, to Carson River; for that was a part of our journey which yet lay shrouded in grim mystery. The directions given us seemed very plain. He traced out the road in the sand with a stick—I think it was his whip handle. It was taken for granted that we knew our way to the 'Sink of the Mary's [Humboldt] River' so he took *that* for his starting point in giving us directions, and showed us that, soon after passing there, we would see a plain wagon track leading to the left, which we were to follow, and it would bring us to grassy meadows, lying two or three miles from the main road, and so, still abounding in feed. Here also, he said, we would find several shallow wells, dug but recently—in the last part of the season—by Mormons, who had gone to spend the winter in California, and on their way there had found these meadows, cut feed in them for use on the forty mile desert and, on arriving in California had given to him and his company—then

1. George R. Stewart, in his excellent book, *The California Trail* (McGraw-Hill, 1962), using data from various sources, calculated that approximately 22,500 people traveled the trail in 1849.
2. Sarah Royce, *A Frontier Lady; Recollections of the Gold Rush and Early California,* ed. Ralph Henry Gabriel (New Haven, Conn.: Yale University Press, 1932). Permission to quote granted. Copyright (c) 1932 by Yale University Press.

AN OXSHOE ON THE TRAIL ON THE EAST SIDE OF HUMBOLDT LAKE

Courtesy Walter Mulcahy
BRADY'S HOT SPRINGS PROVIDED WATER ON THE TRUCKEE
BRANCH OF THE TRAIL.

just about to start for Salt Lake—directions to find the spot.
The wells, he said had good water in them when he was there
a few days before. None of them were deep, but the water
was near the surface all about there, and we could, if we
found it desirable, scoop out one or two of the holes deeper,
let them settle all night, and in the morning have plenty of
fresh water.

"He was evidently an old and experienced traveler of deserts, plains and mountains. He advised us to camp in the
meadows he described, for at least two or three days, let the
cattle rest and feed freely, while the men made it their first
business to cut as much hay as there was room for in the wagon. This would partly dry while the cattle were recruiting;
then load it up, fill every available vessel with water, and set
out on the desert about noon of the day, if the weather were
cool—otherwise toward evening. When once out on the desert we were to stop at intervals of a few hours, feed some of
the hay to the cattle, give them a moderate drink, let them
breathe a short time and then go on. In this way, he said,
we would be able to reach Carson River in about twenty-four
hours from the time of starting on the desert.

"After hearing his instructions, and having the road made
thus plain to us, we went on with renewed cheerfulness and
energy. On Sunday the 16th of September we camped on the
head branch of Mary's River, and on Monday morning passed
through a cañon which brought us to the river itself, down
which we continued to travel for several days. It was now
getting late in the season, and we could not help feeling it
rather ominous that a thunder-storm overtook us one evening
followed by cold nights; and on the evening and night of the
1st of October a terrific wind blew, threatening for hours to
strangle us with thick clouds of sand, and to blow our wagon,
with all our means of living, over the steep bluff. But a good
Providence preserved us and, with the morning calm returned. We had now nearly reached the head of Humboldt
Lake, which, at this late period in the dry season, was utterly
destitute of water, the river having sunk gradually in the sand,
until, hereabout it entirely disappeared. Still, the name, 'Sink

AFTER CROSSING THE FORTY-MILE, EMIGRANTS RESTED HERE AT THE BIG BEND
OF THE TRUCKEE RIVER.

Courtesy Walter Mulcahy

EMIGRANT GRAVEYARD AT WADSWORTH

of Mary's or Humboldt River' was applied in our Guide Book, as well as in conversations at Salt Lake City, to the *southern* or *lower end* of Humboldt Lake, a point some ten miles farther on our way, where, we were told, there were several holes dug, close to the road. Having always understood it to be thus applied, it of course never came into our minds to suppose, that our Mormon friend, when he so particularly marked in the sand 'The Sink of Mary's' meant the point where at that time the river actually disappeared.

"When, therefore, on the night of October 2nd, we camped in the neighborhood of the last mentioned point, we said, 'Now, we must be about twelve or thirteen miles from where that road to the meadows leads off to the left; and thence it will be only two or three miles to the meadows, where we are to rest and prepare for the desert. If we rise very early tomorrow morning, we shall get there by noon, and have a half day to settle camp, and get ready for work.' Accordingly the first one who woke the next morning roused all the rest, and, though we found it not much past two o'clock, we agreed it was not best to sleep again; so, by our fire of sage-brush we took some hot coffee, and the last bit of rabbit pot-pie—the result of a very rare success the day before—yoked up the oxen, and went resolutely on our way.

"It was moonlight, but the gray-white sand with only here and there a sage-brush looked all so much alike that it required care to keep the road. And now, for the first time in my life, I saw a mirage; or several repetitions of that optical illusion. Once it was an extended sheet of water lying calmly bright in the moonlight, with here and there a tree on its shores; and our road seemed to tend directly towards it; then it was a small lake seen through openings in a row of trees, while the shadowy outlines of a forest appeared beyond it; all lying to our left. What a pity it seemed to be passing it by, when our poor animals had been so stinted of late. Again, we were traveling parallel with a placid river on our right; beyond which were trees; and from us to the water's edge the ground sloped so gently it appeared absurd not to turn aside to its brink and refresh ourselves and our oxen.

A WINDSTORM ON THE FORTY-
MILE DESERT.   ➤

"But, as day dawned, these beautiful sights disappeared, and we began to look anxiously for the depression in the ground, and the holes dug, which we were told would mark the Sink of the Humboldt. But it was nearly noonday before we came to them. There was still some passable water in the holes, but not fit to drink clear, so we contrived to gather enough sticks of sage to boil some, made a little coffee, ate our lunch and, thus refreshed, we hastened to find the forking road. Our director had told us, that within about two or three miles beyond the Sink we might look for the road, to the left, and we did look, and kept looking, and going on, drearily, till the sun got lower and lower, and night was fast approaching. Then the conviction, which had long been gaining ground in my mind, took possession of the whole party. We had passed the forks of the road before daylight, that morning, and were now miles out on the desert without a mouthful of food for the cattle and only two or three quarts of water in a little cask.

"What could be done? Halt we must, for the oxen were nearly worn out and night was coming on. The animals must at least rest, if they could not be fed: and, that they might rest, they were chained securely to the wagon, for, hungry and thirsty as they were, they would, if loose, start off frantically in search of water and food, and soon drop down exhausted. Having fastened them in such a way that they could lie down, we took a few mouthfuls of food, and then we in our wagon and the men not far off upon the sand, fell wearily to sleep; a forlorn little company wrecked upon the desert.

"The first question in the morning was, 'How can the oxen be kept from starving?' A happy thought occurred. We had, thus far on our journey, managed to keep something in the shape of a bed to sleep on. It was a mattress-tick, and, just before leaving Salt Lake, we had put into it some fresh hay— not very much, for our load must be as light as possible; but the oid gentleman traveling with us had also a small straw mattress; the two together might keep the poor things from starving for a few hours. At once a small portion was dealt out to them and for the present they were saved. For ourselves we had food which we believed would about last us till we reached the Gold Mines if we could go right on: if we were much delayed anywhere, it was doubtful. The two or three quarts of water in our little cask would last only a few hours, to give moderate drinks to each of the party. For myself I inwardly determined I should scarcely take any of it as, I had found, throughout the journey, that I could do with less drink than most land travelers. Some of the men, however, easily suffered with thirst, and, as to my little girl, it is well known, a child cannot do long without either water or milk. Everything looked rather dark, and dubious.

"Should we try to go on? But there were miles of desert before us, in which, we knew, neither grass or water could be found. We had been told by those who had crossed it with comparatively fresh teams, that, with plenty of hay and water to bait with, we might get over it in about twenty-four hours, though it was acknowledged it might take us longer. Here we were, without water, and with only a few mouthfuls of poor feed, while our animals were already tired out, and very hungry and thirsty. No, it would be madness to go farther out in the desert under such conditions. Should we then turn back and try to reach the meadows with their wells? But, as near as we could calculate, it could not be less than twelve or fifteen miles to them. Would it be possible for our poor cattle to reach there? Their only food would be that pitiful mess still left in our mattresses. It might be divided into two portions, giving them each a few mouthfuls more at noon, and then, if they kept on their feet long enough to reach the holes at the Sink, we might possibly find enough water to give them each a little drink, which, with the remainder of the fodder might keep them up till the meadows were reached. It was a forlorn hope; but it was all we had.

"The morning was wearing away while these things were talked over. Precious time was being wasted; but, the truth was, the situation was so new and unexpected, that it seemed for awhile to confuse—almost to stupefy—most of the little party; and, those least affected in this way, felt so deeply the responsibility of the next move, that they dared not decide upon it hastily. The least responsible and efficient of company had been most of the morning, wandering aimlessly about, sometimes keeping within a small circle, then again branching off nearly out of sight. Perhaps they all had a vague hope they might find another track. But now, as noon approached, they gathered near the wagon, tired, moody, and evidently very near 'giving up.' But this would never do. So the more hopeful ones proposed that we should all eat something and, as soon as the noon heat abated, prepare for a move. So we took some lunch, and soon the men were lying upon the sand at short distances from each other, fast asleep. My little Mary slept too. But I was not sleepy. With unwearied gaze my eyes swept, again and again, the shimmering horizon. There was no help or hope there. Then I looked at what lay nearest. How short-lived our few remaining resources would be, unless fresh strength came soon from somewhere. How still it was. Only the sound of a few feeble breaths. It would not take many hours of starvation to quiet them forever.

"All the human aid we had could do but little now; and if, in trying to do that little, one more mistake were made, it must be fatal. Whence then this calm strength which girded me round so surely, while I, and all surrounding me were so weak? I had known what it was to believe in God, and to pray that He would never leave us. Was it thus then, that when all other helpers failed, He came so near that I no longer simply *believed* in Him, but *knew* His presence there, giving strength for whatever might come? Soon some of the party awoke and, after a little talk, concluded that two of them would walk to a bald ridge that rose out of the flat waste, about a mile and a half distant, and take a view from thence, in the faint hope that we might yet be mistaken, and the forking road and the meadows might still be in advance. My husband said he would go, and the best of the two young men went with him, while the other two wandered listlessly off again. I made no opposition; I felt no inclination to oppose; though I knew the helplessness and loneliness of the position would thus be greatly increased. But that calm strength, that certainty of One near and all sufficient hushed and cheered me. Only a woman who has been alone upon a desert with her helpless child can have any adequate idea of my experience for the next hour or two. But that consciousness of an unseen Presence still sustained me.

"When the explorers returned from their walk to the ridge, It was only to report, no discovery: nothing to be seen on all sides but sand and scattered sagebrush interspersed with the carcasses of dead cattle. So there was nothing to be done but to turn back and try to find the meadows. Turn back! What a chill the words sent through one. *Turn back,* on a journey like that; in which every mile had been gained by most earnest labor, growing more and more intense, until, of late, it had seemed that the certainty of *advance* with every step, was all that made the next step possible. And now for miles we were to *go back.* In all that long journey no steps ever seemed so heavy, so hard to take, as those with which I turned my back to the sun that afternoon of October 4th, 1849.

"We had not been long on the move when we saw dust rising in the road at a distance, and soon perceived we were about to meet a little caravan of wagons. Then a bright gleam of hope stole in. They had doubtless stopped at the meadows, and were supplied with grass and water. Might it not be possible that they would have enough to spare for us? Then we could go on with them. My heart bounded at the thought. But the hope was short lived. We met, and some of the men gathered round our wagon with eager inquiries, while those who could not leave their teams stood looking, with wonder, at a solitary wagon headed the wrong way.

"Our story was soon told. It turned out that they were camping in the meadows at the very time we passed the forking road without seeing it, the morning we so ambitiously started soon after midnight. Ah, we certainly got up too early that day. If we had only seen that road and taken it, we might now have been with this company, provided for the desert, and no longer alone. But, when the question was asked whether they could spare sufficient grass and water to get our team over the desert, they shook their heads, and unanimously agreed that it was out of the question. Their own cattle, they said, were weak from long travel and too often scant supplies. They had only been able to load up barely enough to get to the Carson River. The season was far advanced and the clouds, hanging of late round the mountain tops, looked threatening. It would be like throwing away their own lives without any certainty of saving ours; for once out in the desert without food we would all be helpless together. One of the men had his family with him, a wife and two or three children; and while they talked the woman was seen coming towards us. She had not, when they first halted, understood that any but men were with the lone wagon. As soon as she heard to the contrary, and what were the circumstances, she hastened, with countenance full of concern, to condole with me; and, I think, had the decision depended alone upon her, she would have insisted upon our turning back with them and sharing their feed and water to the last.

"But fortunately for them, probably for us all, other counsels prevailed, and we resumed our depressing backward march. Two or three things, before uncertain, were settled by this meeting. The first was the distance to the meadows, which they agreed could not be less than fourteen or sixteen miles from where we met them, which seemed, in our circumstances, like an appalling interval. But there was relief in being assured that we should find a pretty good supply of water in the holes at the Sink, where we were to camp that night, and that, when we once reached the meadows, there was food and water enough for a number of teams during many days. We had also definite directions as to the shortest road, and were assured it was perfectly plain, and good except that it was rather sandy.

"I had now become so impressed with the danger of the cattle giving out, that I refused to ride except for occasional brief rests. So, soon after losing sight of the dust of the envied little caravan, I left the wagon and walked the remainder of the day. For a good while I kept near the wagon but, by and by, being very weary I fell behind. The sun had set, before we reached the Sink, and the light was fading fast when the wagon

THOSE EMIGRANTS WHO STARTED LATE FACED THE HAZARD OF EARLY WINTER STORMS. ▶

disappeared from my sight behind a slight elevation; and, as the others had gone on in advance some time before, I was all alone on the barren waste. However, as I recognized the features of the neighborhood, and knew we were quite near the Sink, I felt no particular apprehension, only a feeling that it was a weird and dreary scene and instinctively urged forward my lagging footsteps in hope of regaining sight of the wagon.

"Suddenly I caught sight of an object a few rods distant on the left of the road, moving steadily but rather stealthily toward the road, in a line that would intercept it some paces ahead of me. I stopped—the creature stopped too, looking steadily at me. It was a coyote. I had several times during the journey heard them howling at night but, as the season had advanced, they had been seldom heard, and to meet one thus almost face to face with no human being in sight was a little startling. But, calling to mind what I had heard of their reluctance to face a steady look and determined resistance, I lifted my hands with threatening gestures, raised a shout, and sprang forward a step or two. Mr. Coyote stood a moment as if questioning the resistance offered; but when I repeated, more violently, the gestures and the shouts, he turned and retraced his steps into the dim distance, only looking back once or twice to see if the enemy retained the ground. As he disappeared I hastened forward, and in a few minutes came within sight of the wagon, now halted for the night near the camp fire, which the men had just lit.

"The next morning we resumed our backward march after feeding out the last mouthful of fodder. The water in the little cask was nearly used up in making coffee for supper and breakfast; but, if only each one would be moderate in taking a share when thirst impelled him, we might yet reach the wells before any one suffered seriously. We had lately had but few chances for cooking; and only a little boiled rice with dried fruit, and a few bits of biscuit remained after we had done breakfast. If we could only reach the meadows by noon. But that we could hardly hope for, the animals were so weak and tired. There was no alternative, however, the only thing to

be done was to go steadily on, determined to do and endure
to the utmost.

"I found no difficulty this morning in keeping up with the
team. They went so slowly, and I was so preternaturally stim-
ulated by anxiety to get forward, that, before I was aware of
it I would be some rods ahead of the cattle, straining my gaze
as if expecting to see a land of promise, long before I had any
rational hope of the kind. My imagination acted intensely.
I seemed to see Hagar, in the wilderness walking wearily away
from her fainting child among the dried up bushes, and seat-
ing herself in the hot sand. I seemed to become Hagar myself,
and when my little one, from the wagon behind me, called
out 'Mamma I want a drink'—I stopped, gave her some, noted
that there were but a few swallows left, then mechanically
pressed onward again, alone, repeating, over and over, the
words, 'Let me not see the death of the child!'

"Just in the heat of the noon-day we came to where the sage
bushes were nearer together; and a fire, left by campers or
Indians, had spread for some distance, leaving beds of ashes,
and occasionally charred skeletons of bushes to make the scene
more dreary. Smoke was still sluggishly curling up here and
there, but no fire was visible; when suddenly just before me
to my right a bright flame sprang up at the foot of a small
bush, ran rapidly up it, leaped from one little branch to another till all, for a few seconds, were ablaze together, then
went out, leaving nothing but a few ashes and a little smould-
ing trunk. It was a small incident, easily accounted for, but
to my then over-wrought fancy it made more vivid the illusion of being a wanderer in a far off, old time desert, and myself witnessing a wonderful phenomenon. For a few moments
I stood with bowed head worshiping the God of Horeb, and I
was strengthened thereby.

"Wearily passed the hottest noon-day hour, with many an
anxious look at the horned-heads, which seemed to me to bow
lower and lower, while the poor tired hoofs almost refused to
move. The two young men had been out of sight for some-
time; when, all at once, we heard a shout, and saw, a few hundred yards in advance a couple of hats thrown into the air

and four hands waving triumphantly. As soon as we got near enough, we heard them call out, 'Grass and water! Grass and water!' and shortly we were at the meadows. The remainder of that day was spent chiefly in rest and refreshment. The next day the men busied themselves in cutting and spreading grass; while I sorted out and re-arranged things in the wagon so as to make all possible room for hay and water; and also cooked all the meat we had left, and as much of our small stock of flour, rice, and dried fruits, as might last us till we could again find wood.

"The day after that was Sunday, and we should have had a very quiet rest, had we not been visited by a party of some eight or ten Indians, who came from the Humboldt Mountains on Saturday afternoon and remained near us till we left. They professed to be friendly; but were rather troublesome, and evidently desirous of getting something out of us if they could. Two or three of them had rifles; and when the young men went to talk to them they began to show off their marksmanship by firing at particular objects. The young men felt this to be rather of the nature of a challenge; and thought it would be safer to accept than to ignore it. So they got the arms from the wagon, set up a mark, and, as one of them— the gentleman of the two—proved to be a remarkable shot, the Indians were struck with surprise, which, as, time after time, W—'s ball hit within an inch of his aim, grew to admiration, and ended in evident awe; for not one of their party could quite equal him. How much our safety, and exemption from pillage were due to that young man's true aim we might not be quite sure; but I have always been very willing to acknowledge a debt of gratitude to him.

"On Monday morning we loaded up, but did not hurry, for the cattle had not rested any too long; another day would have been better; but we dared not linger. So, giving them time that morning thoroughly to satisfy themselves with grass and water we once more set forward toward the formidable desert, and, at that late season, with our equipment, the scarcely less formidable Sierras. The feeling that we were once more going forward instead of backward, gave an animation to every step which we could never have felt but by contrast. By night we were again at the Sink where we once more camped; but we durst not, the following morning, launch out upon the desert with the whole day before us; for, though it was now the 9th of October, the sun was still powerful for some hours daily, and the arid sand doubled its heat. Not much after noon, however, we ventured out upon the sea of sand; this time to cross or die.

"Not far from the edge of night we stopped to bait, at no great distance from the scene of our last week's bitter disappointment. Once beyond that, I began to feel renewed courage, as though the worst were passed; and, as I had walked much of the afternoon, and knew I must walk again by and by, I was persuaded to get into the wagon and lie down by Mary, who was sleeping soundly. By a strong effort of will, backed by the soothing influence of prayer, I fell asleep, but only for a few minutes. I was roused by the stopping of the wagon, and then my husband's voice said, 'So you've given out, have you Tom?' and at the same moment I knew by the rattling chains and yokes that some of the cattle were being loosed from the team. I was out of the wagon in a minute. One of the oxen was prostrate on the ground, and his companion, from whose neck the yoke was just being removed, looked very likely soon to follow him. It had been the weak couple all along. Now we had but two yoke. How soon would they, one by one, follow?

"Nothing could induce me to get into the wagon again. I said I would walk by the team, and for awhile I did; but by and by I found myself yards ahead. An inward power urged me forward; and the poor cattle were so slow, it seemed every minute as if they were going to stop. When I got so far off as to miss the sound of the footsteps and wheels, I would pause, startled, wait and listen, dreading lest they had stopped, then as they came near, I would again walk beside them awhile, watching, through the darkness, the dim outlines of their heads and horns to see if they drooped lower. But soon I found myself again forward and alone. There was no moon yet, but by starlight we had for some time seen, only too plainly, the dead bodies of cattle lying here and there on both sides of the road. As we advanced they increased in numbers, and presently we saw two or three wagons. At first we thought we had overtaken a company, but coming close, no sign of life appeared. We had candles with us, so, as there was not the least breeze, we lit one or two and examined. Everything indicated a complete break down, and a hasty flight. Some animals were lying nearly in front of a wagon, apparently just as they had dropped down, while loose yokes and chains indicated that part of the teams had been driven on, laden probably with some necessities of life; for the contents of the wagons were scattered in confusion, the most essential articles alone evidently having been thought worth carrying. 'Ah,' we said, 'some belated little company has been obliged to pack what they could, and hurry to the river. Maybe it was the little company we met the other day.' It was not a very encouraging scene but our four oxen still kept their feet; we would drive on a little farther, out of this scene of ruin, bait them, rest ourselves and go on. We did so, but soon found that what we supposed an exceptional misfortune must have been the common fate of many companies; for at still shortening intervals, scenes of ruin similar to that just described kept recurring till we seemed to be but the last, little, feeble, struggling band at the rear of a routed army.

"From near midnight, on through the small hours, it appeared necessary to stop more frequently, for both man and beast were sadly weary, and craved frequent nourishment. Soon after midnight we finished the last bit of meat we had; but there was still enough of the biscuit, rice and dried fruit to give us two or three more little baits. The waning moon now gave us a little melancholy light, showing still the bodies of dead cattle, and the forms of forsaken wagons as our grim waymarks. In one or two instances they had been left in the very middle of the road; and we had to turn out into the untracked sand to pass them. Soon we came upon a scene of wreck that surpassed anything preceding it. As we neared it, we wondered at the size of the wagons, which, in the dim light, looked tall as houses, against the sky. Coming to them, we found three or four of them to be of the make that the early Mississippi Valley emigrants used to call 'Prairie Schooners'; having deep beds, with projecting backs and high tops. One of them was specially immense, and, useless as we felt it to be to spend time in examining these warning relics of those who had gone before us, curiosity led us to lift the front curtain, which hung down, and by the light of our candle that we had again lit, look in. There from the strong, high bows, hung several sides of well cured bacon, much better in quality than that we had finished, at our last resting place. So we had but a short interval in which to say we were destitute of meat, for, though, warned by all we saw not to add a useless pound to our load, we thought it wise to take a little, to eke out our scanty supply of food. And, as to the young men, who had so rarely, since they joined us, had a bit of meat they could call their own, they were very glad to bear the burden of a few pounds of bacon slung over their shoulders.

"After this little episode, the only cheering incident for many hours, we turned to look at what lay round these monster wagons. It would be impossible to describe the motley collection of things of various sorts, strewed all about. The greater part of the materials, however, were pasteboard boxes, some complete, but most of them broken, and pieces of wrapping paper still creased, partially in the form of packages. But the most prominent objects were two or three, perhaps more, very beautifully finished trunks of various sizes, some of them standing open, their pretty trays lying on the ground, and all rifled of their contents; save that occasionally a few pamphlets, or, here and there, a book remained in the corners. We concluded that this must have been a company of merchants hauling a load of goods to California, that some of their animals had given out, and, fearing the rest would they had packed such things as they could, and had fled for their lives toward the river. There was only one thing, (besides the few pounds of bacon) that, in all of these varied heaps of things, many of which, in civilized scenes, would have been valuable, I thought worth picking up. That was a little book, bound in cloth and illustrated with a number of small engravings. Its title was 'Little Ella.' I thought it would please Mary, so I put it in my pocket. It was an easily carried souvenir of the desert; and more than one pair of young eyes learned to read its pages in after years.

"Morning was now approaching, and we hoped, when full daylight came, to see some signs of the river. But, for two or three weary hours after sunrise nothing of the kind appeared. The last of the water had been given to the cattle before daylight. When the sun was up we gave them the remainder of their hay, took a little breakfast and pressed forward. For a long time not a word was spoken save occasionally to the cattle. I had again, unconsciously, got in advance; my eyes scanning the horizon to catch the first glimpse of any change; though I had no definite idea in my mind what first to expect. But now there was surely something. Was it a cloud? It was very low at first and I feared it might evaporate as the sun warmed it. But it became rather more distinct and a little higher. I paused, and stood still till the team came up. Then walking beside it I asked my husband what he thought

THE REMNANTS OF A WAGON RIM ON THE TRAIL ACROSS HUMBOLDT SINK

that low dark line could be. 'I think,' he said, 'it must be the timber on Carson River.' Again we were silent and for a while I watched anxiously the heads of the two leading cattle. They were rather unusually fine animals, often showing considerable intelligence, and so faithful had they been, through so many trying scenes, I could not help feeling a sort of attachment to them; and I pitied them, as I observed how low their heads drooped as they pressed their shoulders so resolutely and yet so wearily against the bows. Another glance at the horizon. Surely there was now visible a little unevenness in the top of that dark line, as though it might indeed be trees. 'How far off do you think that is now?' I said. 'About five or six miles I guess,' was the reply. At that moment the white-faced leader raised his head, stretched forward his nose and uttered a low 'Moo-o-oo.' I was startled fearing it was the sign for him to fall, exhausted. 'What is the matter with him?' I said. 'I think he smells the water' was the answer. 'How can he at such a distance?' As I spoke, the other leader raised his head, stretched out his nose, and uttered the same sound. The

Courtesy Walter Mulcahy
THESE HUMMOCKS SLOWED THE PACE OF WAGONS ON THE CARSON ROUTE

hinder cattle seemed to catch the idea, whatever it was; they all somewhat increased their pace, and from that time, showed renewed animation.

"But we had yet many weary steps to take, and noon had passed before we stood in the shade of those longed-for trees, beside the Carson River. As soon as the yokes were removed the oxen walked into the stream, and stood a few moments, apparently enjoying its coolness, then drank as they chose, came out, and soon found feed that satisfied them for the present, though at this point it was not abundant. The remainder of that day was spent in much needed rest. The next day we did not travel many miles, for our team showed decided signs of weakness, and the sand became deeper as we advanced, binding the wheels as to make hauling very hard. We had conquered the desert."

On October 12, as the Royces were traveling slowly up the Carson River with almost no possibility of successfully crossing the mountains, they were met by two men of a relief party sent out from California to rescue the last of the stragglers of the 1849 migration. And so their hazardous expedition ended fortunately.

During 1850 probably twice the number of people of the preceding year crossed the desert, and their losses of wagons and livestock were almost unbelievable. It is estimated that by the end of the year there were more than 9,000 dead animals and 3,000 abandoned wagons along the Carson River Trail.

By 1852, several small stations had been established on the Humboldt River and in the desert. A journal kept by Mrs. Francis H. Sawyer tells that whiskey sold for two dollars a drink at one of the river way stations and that water on the desert brought seventy-five cents per gallon.

A trading station was built where the trail intercepted the Carson River and was named Ragtown because of the laundry which was washed and hung to dry, or discarded by the thousands who stopped to rest after the hardships of the desert crossing. William A. Wallace, correspondent for the San

A Marker along U.S. Highway 50 Is Almost All That Is Left of Ragtown

A Few Pieces of Rusty Iron and Some Wood Still Mark the Forty-Mile Desert Trail.

Francisco *Alta California* newspaper, traveled from west to east across the Forty-mile in 1858, and he wrote,

"we struck the river again, at dark got supper, and pushed on again, over 20 more miles of desert to Ragtown, once famous for its cotton houses and bad whiskey—where the speculators assembled to buy the weary animals and broken wagons of the emigrants.

"It is said to have at one time contained thirty whiskey shops, and was broken up by famine and disease in 1854. There is a large cluster of graves near by, which are said to have been dug chiefly by bad whiskey. At present near by, Ragtown consists of one house and a blacksmith shop, a watermelon patch and a haystack. . . . This was the last *town*, the last spot dignified with the name and almost the last roof there was to greet our eyes. But we did not regret leaving— we only regretted that we were obliged to tarry there until daylight.

"On the morning of the 8th we started out to cross the desert 40 miles to the Sink. The road there is hard and smooth for the greater portion of the way, but the plain around for thousands of acres together is leafless and lifeless, white arid plains without water, upon which the sun glares. And here, too, over this whole forty miles, are the signs of wrack and ruin which has fallen upon unfortunate emigrants in past years. Heaps of bones lie everywhere, and everywhere are the iron remnants of wagons. It is estimated that ten thousands tons of wagon irons are lying in the sands of that desert; and there are ox chains enough unbroken, to form a continuous line to Salt Lake. This forty miles is the terror of the whole route, and no wonder. These bleaching bones and rusty irons are evidences the sight of which makes one wish to hurry on, and not feel safe until they no longer greet the eye. I never saw a desert before, and I do not wish to see another."

Today there is little left to mark the trails across the Humboldt and Carson Sinks. Here and there one may find a broken bottle, a fragment of pottery or, on the white alkali surface of the playa, tiny crumbs of rusted iron which form an outline of the rim of a wagon wheel. The desert's ancient process of renewing its surface has almost erased the scars of man's great migration across it.

CHAPTER III

The Black Rock Desert —
Indian Stronghold

DESICCATION of the large prehistoric Lake Lahontan, which once covered thousands of square miles of northwestern Nevada, left a great playa—an almost continuous barren flat which stretches for more than one hundred miles in a southwest to northeast direction. Early pioneers divided it into two main parts, to which they attached the names Black Rock and Smoke Creek deserts. It is a spectacular area—a vast, white plain which, although bordered by massive, rugged mountains, appears endless in length. And looking out over it, one can understand the apprehension of the emigrants when they first came to it.

By the end of the first week of August of 1849, thousands of California-bound travelers had already crossed the Humboldt Sink and, following the Truckee and Carson routes, were streaming into the Sacramento Valley. It was during the next week that a company of wagons turned from the Humboldt River trail to travel a route over which Peter Lassen had guided a party the preceding year. Soon hundreds of other wagons were following those tracks.

The migration's sudden change to a new and largely unknown route is understandable. Fear of the Forty-mile Desert, which was not far ahead, and of the high mountains beyond it made the rumor of a new, less hazardous trail the kind of information the weary emigrants desperately wished to believe.

The Lassen route, which was later called the "Death Route" and "Lassen's Horn Route," began at Lassen's Meadows near the headwaters of the present Ryepatch reservoir. From there it traveled in a general westerly direction to Rabbithole Springs and then turned toward the north to cross the Black Rock Desert. Skirting the western edge of the Black Rock

THE GREAT PLAYA, STRETCHING MORE THAN ONE HUNDRED MILES, APPEARS ALMOST
ENDLESS IN LENGTH.

THE BLACK ROCK DESERT DERIVED ITS NAME FROM THIS MOUNTAIN

Range it headed west again at Soldier Meadows to intersect and travel between the towering, sheer walls of the narrow High Rock Canyon. Before reaching Massacre Lake the trail turned to pass through Forty-nine Canyon and on to Surprise Valley, where it climbed over Fandango Pass and down to Goose Lake on the California-Oregon border.

Up to this point, the Lassen route had followed the Applegate trail, over which several companies of wagons had traveled to Oregon during the preceding two years. But at Goose Lake, Lassen had turned south to take his wagons over difficult terrain to the Sacramento Valley.

Instead of being a shortcut to the gold fields, the Lassen route was almost two hundred miles farther than the Carson River and Truckee River routes. The Indians of the northern area were more warlike, and by the time many of the wagons started up the new trail, it was already dangerously late in the season.

Many published and unpublished journals tell of the hardships of those travelers of the Lassen route—of how, believing they were bypassing the dreaded desert of the older trail, they soon learned they would have to cross the equally frightening Black Rock Desert. The accounts were much the same as those of the Forty-mile—the dead and dying livestock along the trail, the deserted wagons, the lack of food and water, the early winter storms which threatened to block the mountain passes.

A great tragedy threatened—and that it did not occur was due to the heroic efforts of rescue parties sent out from California. Because of their self-sacrificial aid, the last of the 1849 travelers of the Lassen route reached the Sacramento Valley during the final week of November.

Three years later another route to California, called Noble's road, followed the old Lassen trail to the hot springs at the Black Rock, turned southwest to skirt the edge of the Black Rock and Smoke Creek deserts, and then passed over the California border into Honey Lake Valley. It was a better, shorter route to northern California; but, during the mid-1860's, its advantages were somewhat offset by the danger of attack by Indians.

THE LASSEN TRAIL TRAVELED BETWEEN THE TOWERING WALLS OF HIGH
ROCK CANYON.

SOME OF THE EARLY TRAVELERS TOOK TIME TO RECORD NAMES AND DATES ON THE
CLIFFS OF HIGH ROCK CANYON.

Driving today along the edge of the great playa, it is easy to believe that it could have been a stronghold for bands of war-like Indians. Cut deep into the surrounding mountains are dark, winding canyons—some of which are almost inaccessible except through narrow passages resembling the gates of a fortress. Small streams and springs offered campsites, and from the high ridges, which jut out into the desert, a sentinel could have watched the dust of an approaching wagon or column of cavalry many miles distant.

Following the two battles of Pyramid Lake[1] in May and June of 1860, a treaty between the Paiute Indians and the whites of northwestern Nevada brought relative peace during the next four years. A band of Smoke Creek Indians, led by a Paiute whom the whites called "Smoke Creek Sam," had broken away from the leadership of the main body of Northern Paiutes and, after the Pyramid Lake war, they continued to steal cattle in Honey Lake Valley and to raid stations on the road along the edge of Black Rock and Smoke Creek deserts. The establishment of a military post at Smoke Creek in the spring of 1863 provided some control of their activities in that area during the last half of 1863 and during 1864.

It was between March of 1865 and January of 1866 that the Black Rock Desert region became the principal battleground for a conflict which, in respect to its ferocity, probably had no equal in Nevada history. Although many early historians have treated it as a series of isolated Indian raids and consequential military reprisals, a study in chronological order of the period's newspaper files and other documents indicates that a savage war, characterized by the hatred of both contestants, suddenly engulfed a large portion of Nevada's northern desert. The lack of attention writers have given to this dramatic conflict and the confusion regarding some of the events is amazing. When the old accounts are pieced together, the story—its plot, its characters, its episodes—becomes the prototype of many novels of the Indian wars.

---

1. Accounts of these two important battles can be read in Thompson and West, *History of Nevada* (1881), and in the reprint, Berkeley, Calif.: Howell-North Books, 1958. Also see Wheeler, *Paiute* (Caldwell, Idaho: The Caxton Printers, Ltd., 1965) and *The Desert Lake* (Caldwell, Idaho: The Caxton Printers, Ltd., 1967).

Early in 1865, according to historian Asa Merrill Fairfield,[2] an expressman was killed north of Smoke Creek, and shortly after the first of March of that year the body of Lucius Arcularius, one of the owners of the Granite Creek Station, was found with two bullet holes in it near Wall Springs. Fairfield pointed out that Arcularius, "known to both white and red men as 'Lucius,' was a man who was liked by everybody. The only fault ever found with him was that he was too kind to Indians. He hired them to work for him and loaned them guns and ammunition with which to hunt rabbits."

Arcularius was robbed and killed by two men, but the records show little evidence that the two men were Indians. During the 1860's there were many whites who murdered men of their own race, and it seems unlikely that the Indians would have selected a man to rob and kill who had befriended them.

However, according to a dispatch sent by several Star City residents to Governor Blasdel, the murder of Arcularius was an "Indian outbreak" which threatened safe passage on the Honey Lake to Humboldt road, an important route in 1865.

At sunrise on the same day of the Star City dispatch, but unrelated to it, an event which may have been the catalyst for the ensuing long and brutal conflict took place on an unofficial but generally recognized Indian reservation.

According to his military report, Captain A. B. Wells and his fifty men of Company D, Nevada Volunteers, arrived at Pyramid Lake on the evening of March 13 and there received information that a band of Indians, suspected of stealing cattle, were encamped about eleven miles north at Winnemucca (Mud) Lake. At three o'clock the next morning, with thirty-one men, Captain Wells started for the Indian camp—arriving in sight of it two and one-half hours later.

Dividing his command into three squads, he advanced on the Indians, "intending to arrest them, but when within about one hundred and fifty yards, they commenced firing upon me. The first shot took effect in Corporal Dolan's shoulder, wounding him slightly; the second passed through the cape

2. Asa Merrill Fairfield, *Fairfield's Pioneer History of Lassen County, California*, (San Francisco: H. S. Crocker Co., 1916).

VICTIMS OF AN INDIAN RAID ON A WAGON TRAIN ARE BELIEVED BURIED IN THIS MULTIPLE GRAVE NEAR THE LASSEN TRAIL.

A SECTION OF THE TRAIL BETWEEN LASSEN MEADOWS AND RABBITHOLE

REMNANT OF A SHEEPHERDER'S OUTFIT RESTS NEAR THE HOT SPRINGS BELOW
THE BLACK ROCK.

THE MOUNTAINS BORDERING THE BLACK ROCK DESERT PROVIDED STRONGHOLDS FOR
INDIAN WAR PARTIES.

of my overcoat. I then ordered a charge with sabres . . . and a general engagement ensued. The Indians fought like veterans. I killed twenty-nine in all; but one escaped."

It was a strange report—twenty-nine Indian warriors, who "fought like veterans," were killed in an engagement in which only one white suffered a slight wound from the first shot fired. And yet the Indians were of the same tribe which, five years before at the battle of Pyramid Lake, had easily defeated a volunteer army of one hundred and five white men.

Three days later, the Virginia City *Daily Union* newspaper commented, "We learn that Captain Jim, of the Washoe tribe . . . expressed the belief that Captain Wells had attacked and killed a party of thirty innocent Washoes, who recently went on a fishing expedition to that locality. . . . For humanity's sake, we hope this supposition is not true."

The *Daily Union's* suggestion of such a possibility was immediately attacked by Virginia City's *Territorial Enterprise* and this touched off a heated debate between the two newspapers.

THE CURRENTLY DRY WINNEMUCCA LAKE (IN BACKGROUND) WAS CALLED MUD LAKE IN 1865.

On March 23, Governor Blasdel, accompanied by an army escort, traveled to Fort Churchill to meet with "twenty-five or thirty Chiefs and Captains" of the Paiute Indians, and a council was held the following day. According to the Virginia City *Daily Union* reporter who attended, Young Winnemucca (Numaga)[3] stated that the camp was taken by surprise and among the dead were sixteen to eighteen women and children. He said that the Indians who stole the cattle were not in the camp at the time of attack.

The *Territorial Enterprise* of March 25 charged, "That such a dispatch should have been transmitted to the (Daily) Union is not at all strange, for the reporter who furnished it was sent expressly to Fort Churchill to hunt up further Piute[4] proof in support of the peculiar position of that journal."

---

3. Young Winnemucca (Numaga) was highly respected by the whites of Nevada. In 1860 he had attempted to prevent the Pyramid Lake war; but when the whites attacked, he led the Indians to victory. It was Numaga who, with Colonel Frederick Lander, made the treaty between the Paiutes and the whites in August of 1860.

4. In early days Paiute was often written "Piute," "Pi-Ute," "Pa-ute," or "Pah-ute."

Courtesy Nevada State Highway Department
FORT CHURCHILL, ON THE CARSON RIVER, WAS ESTABLISHED IN 1860

The *Daily* responded by claiming that its reporter had been invited to the council, and went on to comment:

"The report of Capt. Wells is that the men killed in the fight were Smoke Creek Indians. Winnemucca (Numaga) says they were some of his people—mostly women and children. It is ascertained upon corroborative evidence that the two wives of old Winnemucca (Poito)[5] were slain in this 'stubborn and sanguinary' battle, where the killing was all on one side. Do they belong to the Smoke Creek Indians? If not, how came they among them? Captain Wells, in his report, says nothing about the killing of women; but he does say that he destroyed the arms captured from the Indians. Why destroy them? Where there was such a 'stubborn and sanguinary' fight between about equal forces, the Indians must have had guns, pistols, and knives, and these should have been brought in and turned over to the commander at Fort Churchill. Arms are useful, and when taken from the enemy are the property of the Government. It seems to your reporter that it would have been a very easy matter for Capt. Wells to have brought these trophies back with him, as it appears from the Enterprise of Friday, that his command did bring in some trophies of that battle. The following is copied from that paper:

" 'INDIAN SCALPS,—Notwithstanding orders to the contrary, it is said that Capt. Wells' men (Company D), who were in the fight at Mud Lake, took fourteen or fifteen scalps. One of the men claims to have the scalp of the Notorious Smoke Creek Sam. . . .' "

On March 26, Major Charles McDermit, commander of all army troops in Nevada, wrote to Governor Blasdel and Captain Wells: "Mr. Gilson, Sub- (Indian) Agent on the Truckee, arrived last night. From his report, thirty-two (32) Indians were killed by Captain Wells. All were men but two. A large number were from Smoke Creek. It was the right stroke in the right place, from what I can learn."

---

5. Old Winnemucca (Poito) was not related to Young Winnemucca (Numaga).

This provided the *Enterprise* with an editorial which stated in part, "The above clashes somewhat with the Piute statement of the Union. According to the story of that journal, sixteen or seventeen women were killed . . . , and Capt. Wells and his company reveled in a carnival of innocent blood. . . . We trust the Union will require no additional evidence in proof of the injustices of its charges against Capt. Wells and his company. A great wrong has been done, and the injury should be repaired by a prompt retraction."

The *Daily Union* quickly responded. After quoting the accusations of the *Enterprise*, it summarized its beliefs and asked several pertinent questions.

"The above is from the Enterprise of yesterday. As it and its correspondents appear exceedingly anxious that we shall condemn Captain Wells, we will now say more than we have heretofore said in regard to the 'desperate hand-to-hand' fight he recently had with the Indians at Mud Lake. Thus far, the extent of our charges against Captain Wells have consisted in giving publicity to assertions made by the Indians. We never vouched for the truth of those assertions; but we will now say that we believe they are, in the main, too true for the future welfare of the Captain, if the matter undergoes that thorough investigation which it merits and which we sincerely trust it will receive. We now call upon Gov. Blasdel and Major McDermit to sift this affair to the bottom, and place Captain Wells before the public in his true position. If he performed his duty, and nothing more, a thorough investigation will suit him exactly. If he murdered a band of innocent Indian men, women, and children, let him suffer the consequences, and lose his epaulets. It is our opinion that Major McDermit and Captain Wells friends desire to hush this matter up. If they succeed in doing so, they will doubtless again hear from us and some of their Pi-Ute friends.

"The Enterprise trusts 'the Union will require no additional evidence in proof of the injustice of its charges against Captain Wells and his company.' Previous to this time, we have made no charges against Captain Wells and his company;

but from the evidence now before us, we must say that it looks to us just as if he made a most egregious blunder when he attacked those Indians at Mud Lake, and that time will prove it.

"The above dispatch, from Major McDermit, says Gilson, sub-agent on the Truckee, reports thirty-two Indians killed, all men but two—that a large number were from Smoke Creek, and that it was the right stroke in the right place, *from what he can learn.* There is where we differ with the Major. We have had access to as much information on the subject as he has, and *from what we can learn, it was a stroke in the wrong place.* We had a conversation with Gilson after he visited Fort Churchill and made his report to Major McDermit, and he stated to us that *twenty-nine* Indians were killed, (among them two of old Winnemucca's wives) ; that not a single white man had been on the battle-ground since the fight; that the fight was a desperate one; that *probably half* those killed were Smoke Creek Indians, and that *his information was derived from Indians* whom he sent out to bury the dead. Why did Gilson not go with the Indians to bury the dead? Was it because he expected to find a number of women and children among the slain, and did not wish to place himself in a position to testify against Capt. Wells and his company? It seems to us that it was his duty to superintend the interment of the bodies, and then make a report to headquarters based upon what he knew from personal observation, and not upon what the Indians told him, unless we are going to settle the whole matter by Indian testimony, which, when it comes through Gilson, appears to be acceptable to Major McDermit and our contemporary; but when it comes from one of the same Indians, directly through one of our reporters, it is worthless.

"Our readers will remember that this was represented as a 'desperate hand-to-hand fight.' When Gilson admitted to us that two women were killed, we asked him what excuse there was for killing them, when he replied that they were shot at so great a distance—a half a mile or more—that it was impossible to distinguish the squaws from the bucks. Now, that must have been a very desperate hand-to-hand fight, where the combatants were so far apart that it was impossible to distinguish men from women. When we asked Gilson what Winnemucca's wives were doing in a camp of the Smoke Creeks, he did not pretend to claim that all of the Indians were Smoke Creeks, but he thought that probably half of them were, for the Indians told him so.

"We have heard it rumored that, in addition to the murder of several children in that 'desperate' fight, two or three little ones were thrown into the river and allowed to drown, and the Enterprise recently stated that *fourteen or fifteen scalps were taken*. Now, those are stories that need looking into, and after so much has been said, not half of which has been published, there is only one way in which this affair can be settled to the credit or discredit of Capt. Wells and that is by the Governor, and Major McDermit giving it a thorough investigation, which we shall insist upon until it is had."[6]

It is unlikely that more than a century later there is sufficient evidence to state with certainty the truth of what occurred at Winnemucca Lake; but it is obvious that, for many years, the Indians of northern Nevada believed that innocent people of their race had been deliberately massacred. As late as 1883, in her book *Life Among the Piutes*, Sarah Winnemucca wrote, "It was all old men, women and children that were killed."

As late as March 25, 1865, the *Humboldt Register* newspaper of Unionville was optimistic about future Indian troubles in Humboldt County.

"THE INDIAN ALARM.—Dispatches have been sent to the Governor, representing that settlers and travelers along the road between this county and Susanville have been put to much trouble, and one or two killed, by Indians. These statements were correct; and we are glad to be informed that the Governor has taken measures to afford the people along that road the protection asked.

"It may be well to state, however, for the satisfaction of persons who have friends here, or acquaintances who owe

_____
6. See Appendix B, par. A.

them coin, within the meaning of the specific contract law, that in Humboldt county we are not dwelling in the midst of alarms; that we have had no trouble with the Indians, except that from places remote from the principal towns stock in considerable numbers has been stolen. In the Upper Humboldt region, there is greater danger. We are told that Major McDermit intends establishing a post in or near Paradise Valley, to be occupied by a company of cavalry. Paradise Valley is a point where several much-traveled roads approach. An establishment there, even of but one good mounted company, will afford ample protection for the settlers and roads throughout a wide extent of country. Forage is abundant there, and provisions can be taken over an excellent wagon road at all times of year. From there mounted men can in a few hours reach any point in the Humboldt country likely to be annoyed by the vagabond Indians roving from the Black Rock country to the Susanville road.

"In all the towns of this county a chronic quiet reigns, and people feel secure under their scalps. Some alarm was occasioned, the other day, by the discovery that the squaws and young Piutes had been removed from the canyons; but that has worn off, and all feel secure."

On approximately the same day this editorial was being written an Indian walked into the Granite Creek station on the edge of the Black Rock desert and asked for Lucius Arcularius. One of the four white men there, a visitor named Waldron, picked up a gun, put it to the Indian's face, and told him to look into the barrel. When the Indian obeyed, the white man pulled the trigger.

A few days later burning revenge swept down upon the station and its three occupants—A. Curry, C. Creele, and A. Simmons. The April 15 issue of Unionville's *Humboldt Register* newspaper told of the hatred the red avengers brought with them.

"On the 7th, a small party . . . left Unionville for a reconnaisance of a portion of the Honey Lake road. They overtook and joined another party, thirteen men from settlements along the river, out on the same mission. On the 9th, the party reached Granite Creek Station. . . . On the 1st of April, a large column of smoke was seen rising from the vicinity, and the supposition is the station was that day attacked by the Indians. The walls of the house occupied by the men were built very thick, of sod. They had made ten loop-holes, for their rifles, on the side attacked. The attack was made from a stone corral about 30 paces off, in front of the house. The whole front of the corral is bespattered with lead of the bullets fired from the house. By appearances, the fight is supposed to have lasted about half-a-day. Curry was killed by a shot through a loop-hole—a body found in the house having been recognized by persons acquainted with him. The legs, from below the knees, were missing.

"The Indians must have exhausted their ammunition, for they fired long missiles before leaving, made from the screw ends of wagon bolts, cut about an inch long and partially smoothed. Two of these were found—one in a bellows near the house, and the other planted two inches deep in wood. Near the lodging-place of the latter was a blood stain, and it is supposed the missile had killed a dog belonging to the place —a savage animal, intolerant of Indians. His skin was tanned, but left on the ground.

"The Indians gained possession of a store-house, adjoining the dwelling, by tearing out a wall. This enabled them to reach the roof, and then it is supposed that Creele and Simmons resorted to flight—taking that desperate chance in preference to burning. Creele struck out across the flat towards Hot Springs. The flat is of alkali, very wet, and the tracks are left plain. Three Indians, two on horses and one on a mule, pursued and captured him. Brought him back to the house; and all the indications attest that he was burned to death. A portion of the skull, a jawbone, and some small pieces of bone were found; the other portions of the body having been reduced to ashes. At the point where the arms would be, were large rocks piled up, everything indicating that he had been thus weighted down; and then a large pile of sawed lumber was built up over him—stubs of the lumber still remaining when these marks were found—and the poor fellow thus burnt up.

"Simmons took to the road leading to Deep Hole Station. He ran about 30 or forty rods, and there the mark of a pool of blood denotes that he fared not quite so badly—having been shot down. The body was dragged off a short distance, and much mutilated. The remains of all the men, such as were found, were buried by this party on the 9th."

The Granite Creek Station attack was the beginning of a series of Indian raids and military retaliations which took the lives of many people during the next ten months. The 1865 and 1866 reports do not provide comprehensive information regarding the identity of the Indian tribes involved in the engagements or the organization of the bands. Most early historians concluded that the war parties were made up of Paiutes, Bannocks (whom the Paiutes called their cousins), and possibly some Shoshoni.[7]

---

7. See Appendix B, par. B.

THE REMAINS OF THE GRANITE CREEK STATION CAN STILL BE SEEN APPROXIMATELY FIVE MILES NORTH OF GERLACH.

The prominence of the name of Black Rock Tom in almost everything written during this period indicates that he was one of the leaders; and, as a dramatic Indian war chief, he could have stepped out of a twentieth-century motion picture. The *Humboldt Register* commented, "All hunters of Indians, who came to an engagement anywhere between this and Owyhee, and almost all parties attacked on that road, during the past season, remarked a white horse of extraordinary qualities, the rider of which seemed to take great pride in his efforts to 'witch the world with noble horsemanship.' The white horse was ever spoken of as a wonder of strength and fleetness. His rider, a stalwart Indian, delighted to dally just out of musket range from the white men, caricoling most provokingly, and darting off, occasionally, with the fleetness of the wind. The rider was 'Black Rock Tom.' "

On the fifth of April, only a few days after the Granite Creek Station raid, a party of twenty-five Indians surrounded a ranch house in Paradise Valley. One of the three white men in the house managed to escape and rode to warn other settlers

THE INDIANS FIRED AT THE MEN IN THE GRANITE CREEK STATION FROM BEHIND THE WALLS OF THIS CORRAL.

—advising them to go to a ranch where a corral made of sod would provide a fort.

In danger of being cut off, nine men, four women, and ten children from nearby ranches were soon hurrying for the corral, and the mental condition of at least one of them was described in the *Humboldt Register:*

"One man who had been laid up for weeks with inflammatory rheumatism, not able to touch a foot to the ground, was being drawn on two wheels by his friends. When he saw the danger, he forgot he was lame—and jumped from the cart and ran as swift as the swiftest; but as soon as the excitement was over he could not bear up his own weight."

On reaching the improvised fort, the settlers were surrounded by approximately seventy-five Indians. One of the party on a fast horse managed to break through the circle of attackers and reach the settlement of Willow Point, twelve miles distant. When he returned with reinforcements three hours later, the Indians retreated and the next morning left the valley with four hundred head of cattle and horses. When a rescue party finally reached the ranch house first attacked, they found it burned and its two occupants dead.

Late in March, Major McDermit sent a detachment of troops commanded by a Lieutenant Wolverton to Humboldt County, and less than two weeks later ordered Captain Wells and his company to proceed there. Unionville's *Humboldt Register* of April 15 reported, "Captain Wells, with 108 mounted men, arrived here Wednesday afternoon, on their way to Paradise Valley—where he will rendevouz for a while, taking care of the thieving Indians in the surrounding country. Wells is a clever fellow, seeming quite civilized. Had no Indian scalps at his belt—didn't even have a large, tanned scalp, with the 'dander' well up: which we expected him to bring from Virginia. Didn't give any savage war whoop as he landed; but put his boys through a bit of circus performance, by talking square English to them, and then quit them, and took a smile with sundry civilians, much the same as a

PARADISE VALLEY ABOUT THE TURN OF THE CENTURY

UNIONVILLE'S WELLS FARGO BUILDING IN 1885

bloodless militia Captain in the States would have done. The
Virginia Union has made a mistake in Wells: He is a very
modest, civil fellow—and we wouldn't be afraid to go on a
fishing excursion in his neighborhood.

"The Soldiers are a fine looking company, and the best
armed of any on this coast; having the customary carbine and
saber, and in addition almost every man is supplied with one
of Colt's Army revolvers. They behaved well while here—no
complaint whatever could be heard against them. Before
cooking their supper, almost every man of the command took
a bath in the creek. 'Cleanliness is akin to godliness'—and we
don't believe these fellows will disturb any godly sort of Indian.

"The horses are generally good ones though, not in quite
as good condition as stock which was Wintered out here.

"Capt. Wells will have, when he gets them together, 155
men. His headquarters will be at Paradise Valley—from which
point he will be able to watch over that section, now rapidly
settling, and protect settlers and teamsters on the Honey Lake
road. A part of his force will pursue, with all haste, the band
of Indians which has gone towards Black Rock with a band of
stock numbering near a thousand head, horses and cattle."

During the following month Indian raids continued; one
of which on May 4, occurred only fifteen miles from Unionville. A letter in the May 13 *Humboldt Register* complained,
"The Indians seem so far to have plenty of ammunition, and
it has been asserted by many who pretend to know, that they
keep their supply good from purchases they make in Austin.
. . . It is to be hoped, if there is any truth in this statement,
that the good citizens of Austin will mete out the same pun-
ishment upon any found selling ammunition to them that
they would to a Piute or Shoshone caught in the act of murder."

A month after his arrival, Captain Wells was again making
news, but according to the *Register* he was finding his foe
more difficult to conquer.

"On the afternoon of the 20th, at a point 25 miles east of Clover Valley—about 125 miles northeast from Unionville—Capt. Wells, with 70 men, came upon the Indians, who were in a strongly fortified position. A fight ensued, which lasted four hours. The Indians were well armed, and defended the position with great bravery. Wells charged their works repeatedly, but was each time repulsed.

"Two men—privates Godfrey and Monroe—fell within 30 feet of the works, and their bodies and arms were captured by the Indians. At dark, Wells withdrew. It appeared, by observations from camp that night, that the soldiers were completely surrounded. The enemy's camp fires blazed on every side. Wells determined on a retreat. He buried his ammunition, and retired at a gallop. His command is up on the river. Wells went on yesterday's stage for Carson, expecting to be back in 8 days with howitzers. He estimates the Indian force at five or six hundred, and thinks he killed twenty to twenty-five. Three of his men were wounded."

The *Register* hinted at the fear of defeat which the strength of Indian forces was bringing to the whites of northern Nevada.

"A few more retreats, and Indian hunting will be conducted with white people in the lead—Indians pursuing. It is unfortunate. Captain Wells undoubtedly did just what he thought was necessary. The necessity was a great misfortune —we pray it may not prove a calamity—to our people."

On July 8, after an attack in the Quinn (Queen's) River region on a party of eighteen men and three wagons, the *Register* expressed its disappointment in the army's conduct of the war.

"We have to chronicle another attack of Indians on persons who started on the Boise road, deluded with the belief that Col. McDermit's command of 600 men, which has been out that way this long time, afforded full security against the Indians . . . why shall not the shortest route between California

PHOTOGRAPH OF FORT MCDERMIT TAKEN IN 1887

and Idaho be cleared of these murdering devils? We dislike to complain of the military; believing that Col. McDermit means to do what is right. . . ."[8]

A month and four days later, August 12, the same newspaper printed the following, "Colonel McDermit, commanding the troops on the Upper Humboldt, went out, some days ago, with a small scouting party, looking for Indians. Returning, on the 6th inst., when near Queen's River, the party was surprised by Indians in ambush. Two others were wounded, and Col. McDermit shot in the breast; from the effects of which he died, in 4 hours. . . .

"Col. McDermit was a candid, straightforward, kind-hearted man. His men were devoted to him; and the tidings of his death caused tears to well from many a manly eye; and many a man in that little army resolved anew to wreak a fear-

8. See Appendix B, par. D.

COLONEL CHARLES McDERMIT AND HIS FAMILY

ful vengeance upon the murdering red devils who infest the border. The deceased, we understand, leaves a wife and two children, at Fort Churchill."

Five days later, the *Humboldt Register* revealed the state of anxiety of some of Unionville's citizens—who advocated the killing of all members of the town's Indian colony.

"Capt. Wells, with Lieut. Wolverton and 84 men . . . started yesterday morning for Fort Churchill.

"We do not understand why troops are called away at this time. The country about the Upper Humboldt and Queen's River is overrun and held by murdering Indians. Never yet has the force up there been one-fourth as strong as it should be. Hill Beachy is now on his way to San Francisco, to make statement as to the necessity of greater protection to the Idaho road. All the roads in danger from Indians when Wells was sent out are as bad now. The last Indian camp he struck was of a large, well-provisioned and well-armed band, only over in Golconda, between this and Reese River, and Wells did not get a scalp. Murdering stragglers keep up a communication with non-participating but sympathizing Indians here. It is even now in discussion among our people, whether or not it were good policy and the only security against the Indians, to deliberately put out the light of the 'friendly' band managed here by Capt. Sou—on the ground that he and his people manifestly have continual intercourse with the murdering bands, affording them information, giving them aid and comfort, nursing their wounded, and furnishing them occasionally with a man."

Apparently fearing that the hostilities would eventually result in the destruction of the entire Paiute tribe, Captain Sou decided to aid the cavalry, and it may have been this decision, providing the army with competent Indian scouts, which turned the tide of the war. The *Register* of September 9 tells how Sou and two other Paiutes guided the troops to a successful attack on an Indian camp in the Table Mountain region; and during the same month at a place described as twenty miles northwest of Buffalo Spring in Queen's River Valley, an Indian camp, located by the light of its cooking fires, was surprised and thirty-five Indians were killed. The account of the fight states, "One horse, which had often before attracted notice, was again conspicuous on this occasion—a white animal, that defied all efforts to approach his rider."

Another sentence in the report will be of interest to those who do, or do not, believe that Nevada Indians poisoned their arrowpoints. "Among the spoils taken . . . was also found a preparation for poisoning arrows—supposed to consist of beef's liver impregnated with the venom of the rattlesnake."[9]

On November 4, an Indian war party led by Black Rock Tom attacked a freight wagon proceeding along the road from the Black Rock Desert to the Humboldt River. The driver was killed and mutilated and the wagon burned. It was this

---

9. See Appendix A.

Courtesy Nevada Historical Society
FOURTEEN-HORSE AND MULE-TEAM WAGONS CARRYING FREIGHT ALONG AN EARLY
NORTHERN NEVADA ROAD.

TODAY, LITTLE REMAINS OF DUN GLEN

minor raid which eventually resulted in the destruction of
Black Rock Tom's band and his death.

Guided by Captain Sou, a force of twenty-five soldiers from
Dun Glen under the command of a Lieutenant Penwell set
out in pursuit of the Indian band. They found it well en-
trenched in the mountains of the Black Rock Range near
Paiute Creek, and after an unsuccessful attack in which neither side suffered casualties, Lieutenant Penwell and his men
returned to Dun Glen.

According to the *Register*, a second expedition against the
Black Rock desert stronghold was better prepared. "Lieut.
Osmer, on the morning of the 13th inst., started after the savages with a force of 60 soldiers, 4 citizens, and 8 friendly Indians headed by Capt. Sou.

"Sou's fidelity to the whites, and zeal in their cause, in connection with the success that has uniformly attended his
efforts in aid of the soldiers, entitle him to the gratitude of
our people, as well as to a considerable degree of their con-
fidence.

"On reaching the sink of Queen's River (Black Rock desert), 100 miles northwest of Dun Glen, Lieut. Osmer left his
wagons in charge of a guard of 14 men, and taking two days
cooked rations, set out for the point where the Indians were
supposed to be. His force then consisted of 46 soldiers, 4
citizens, and the 8 Piutes. After overcoming almost insuper-
able obstacles, in crossing the slough formed by the sink of
Queen's river during a very dark night, on the morning of
the 17th the Piute guides said they could see the smoke of an
Indian encampment at a point about 9 miles distant; and
they were very positive in asserting that it was that of Capt.
Tom's (Black Rock Tom) band, which it was supposed
murdered Bellew. Although none of the whites could see
any smoke, or other evidence of the existence of any Indian
camp in that locality, until after getting within 5 miles of it,
having faith in the superior discernment of their Indian
allies they went forward, fully prepared for the sanguinary
work upon which they were soon to enter.

The savages did not discover the approach of the command,

PART OF THE LONG BARN OF THIS RANCH IN PARADISE VALLEY WAS ONE OF THE FORT WINFIELD SCOTT BUILDINGS.

until it was within 2 miles of their camp; when they at once secreted themselves behind bushes and the banks of a creek in the vicinity, and, on the arrival of the troops, they fought with desperation. The soldiers were trammeled with no formal commands. The only order given by Osmer was 'Come on, boys!' and then, with an energy that seemed irresistible, the boys in blue, the citizens, and the friendly Indians, every one for himself, but with admirable system, entered upon the contest—each striving to surpass the others in deeds of daring. The Indians were well armed, with guns, and bows and arrows. Their arrows are dangerous weapons—having sharp iron and steel points, some of which are poisoned.

"The number of Indians known to have been killed is about 55,[10] and it is safe to infer that a considerable number of their killed were not found; for the fight lasted about four hours,

---

10. See Appendix B, par. C.

and extended over an area of about three miles square full of gullies and covered with sage and other brush.

"One of the soldiers, named David O'Connell, was killed —being shot in the breast with a large iron slug; and two were painfully, but not mortally wounded."

Other sources[11] reported that, "After the battle was over a corporal was called by a comrade as he was coming down the side of the mountain. He went to him and found him trying to stop the blood that was flowing from the wounds of an Indian mother. Beside her lay an infant that had been struck by an accidental shot and near by was another child about two years old. The private wanted the corporal to help him carry the squaw down to the camp, for he thought it was too bad to let her die and the children starve. The corporal said he was in a hurry and told him to call a citizen nearby to help him. Soon after reaching the foot of the hill he heard several pistol shots in the direction of where he had left the two men and the squaw, and looking up that way saw the soldier coming down alone. When he came up the corporal said, 'Where is that squaw?' 'That was a fine specimen you called to help me,' was the reply. 'The —— bush-whacker shot the whole lot of them, babies and all, before I knew what he was up to.' "

Black Rock Tom was one of the few Indians who managed to escape, and after the destruction of his band, he apparently went to the Humboldt Sink. On December 30, the *Humboldt Register* reported, "Several messengers have come, lately, from Capt. Sou to citizens here, asking them to come down to the Big Meadows and be put in possession of the notorious cut-throat known as 'Black Rock Tom.' Those who have been accustomed to attend to such business were busy, and Tom remained on the Meadows, doubtless feeling each day more secure. Then Capt. Street came that way, Tuesday, Sou notified him of the opportunity to capture this leading marauder. Street took him in charge, and gave him in keeping to a squad of his boys, with particular instruction not to permit an es-

---

11. *Fairfield's Pioneer History of Lassen County* and other early histories of Nevada record this incident.

cape. Soon after Tom attempted to escape, and several musket balls flew through his chest in an instant. Tom will murder no more travelers."

Another article in the same paper of that date included:
"He has quit this vale of tears; but the horse has not been
taken. Tom did not bring the pale horse on his last trip, and
so the noble and much-coveted animal is still in Indian hands."

The final large battle of the Black Rock Desert was fought
on January 12, 1866—and it was the most spectacular of all.
Containing so many of the elements and characters of a modern drama, a nonfiction writer would hesitate to use the story
except as a direct quotation. And it is doubtful that rewriting
could improve the original version published in the *Humboldt Register* on January 20, 1866.

"A Gallant Fight In Fish Creek Valley.—One of the best
fights yet recorded since the Indians of our northern border
commenced hostilities, was made near the confluence of
Queen's River and Fish creek[12] last week. We give a somewhat
extended and correct account of the expedition, as being
a remarkable triumph over terrible hardships incident to bad
weather, and as being more interesting to our readers than any
other matter with which the account might be replaced. The
gallant officer who had charge of the campaign—the brave
soldiers who sprang like electric sparks from the chrysalis state
into which the ice was reducing them when the order 'forward' was given—the gallant citizens, who gave up the ease
and comfort of town life to hunt the common enemy—and
even the Piutes, who attest their friendship by secretly guid-

---

12. Extensive research of documents and maps of the 1860's has not located a Fish
Creek or Fish Creek Valley in the vicinity of Queen's (Quinn) River. With the aid
of Jim Bidart of the Leonard Creek ranch, and other persons familiar with the area,
the distances and descriptions provided by the *Humboldt Register* have been thoroughly studied. The article states, "The Indian encampments were on the western
side of Fish creek Valley, about 60 miles west of Paradise Valley." This distance and
direction would place them somewhere in the northern section of the Black Rock
Desert where three streams—Battle and Bartlett creeks from the west and Leonard
Creek from the north—flow from the mountains down into the desert. The area
into which Battle Creek flows is separated from the main desert by low mountains
and could have been considered a different valley. It is wondered if the battle of
January 12 gave Battle Creek its name.

ing the white man to the enemy's camps—all earned our gratitude.

"The Indians had become so daring and troublesome, of late, that communication between Dun Glen and Camp McDermit was unsafe. The Queen's river region was dangerous. (Is yet, for that matter.) Capt. G. D. Conrad, of Company B, Second Cal. Vol. Cavalry, determined on a raid against the marauders. The campaign having been planned and all preparations made, the command set out from Dun Glen on the morning of the 8th, headed for Queen's river. The force was composed as follows: Of Co. B, 35 men; citizens, 9; Piutes, 12. We have been furnished by Mr. W. K. Parkinson, of the expedition, the particulars as they transpired—substantially as follows:

"Night of the 9th, camped at Willow Point Station, Paradise Valley. Remained there until the evening of the 10th, and made a night march over the mountains into the Queen's river Valley, in order to enter the Valley unobserved; and

Looking South from Leonard Creek. The Mountains beyond the Dog's Head Separate the Eastern Section of the Desert from the Area into which Battle Creek Flows.

camped at Cane Springs. Capt. Conrad, Thos. Ewing, and Sergeant Korble, having gone ahead during the day and ascended a high Mountain Peak, commanding a view of the Valley of Queen's river, kept a sharp lookout for fires until 9 o'clock at night; and no fires appearing, the Captain correctly concluded that the Indians had left the valley—the weather being so very cold that fire was a necessity. During the night the command was joined by a detachment of 25 men from Company I, same regiment, commanded by Lieut. Duncan accompanied by Dr. Snow, a citizen physician.

"On the morning of the 11th, it having snowed during the night, and the morning being very cold and stormy, the snow blowing in clouds, the command was in motion as soon as it was light enough to see, marching towards Queen's river, 20 miles distant. Reached the river in the afternoon, and after much difficulty found a deep hole in the river that was not frozen solid, and cut through the ice and camped. The water was so full of sulphur and decayed matter that the horses would not drink it, and the men were compelled to melt the ice to get water with which to make coffee. That night Capt. Conrad, with four soldiers, Parkinson, Ewing, and Indians Sou and Bob, went on a scout; and after a cold and difficult ride of 7 miles in a westerly direction from the camp, they reached the summit of a range of mountains lying between Queen's river Valley and Fish creek Valley, from which point they had a view of Fish creek Valley for thirty miles. They discovered fires in a northwesterly direction, and on the further side of Fish creek Valley—as nearly as they could determine, about 12 miles from the base of the mountain on which they stood. Capt. Sou thought from the appearance of the fires that there were a great many warriors, and that the command would have a hard fight. The Captain took bearings and directions as well as could be done under the circumstances, and determined to make the attack at daylight on the following morning. The scouting party returned to camp, and the order was given for the command to be in the saddle at half-past 11 o'clock. The brave boys in blue received the announcement with joy. Then followed the bustle and preparation for battle: supper at 10 o'clock; horses fed; extra ammunition issued; pack train and wagons ordered to follow at daylight.

"Precisely at half-past 11 o'clock the order to march was given, and the entire command formed in line. Capt. Conrad gave the necessary orders, forbidding indiscriminate slaughter of women and children, and the command commenced the long, cold march of 20 miles. The night was dark and stormy. Having to cross Fish creek, and there being many hot springs along that stream, making it miry in the coldest weather, an early start was necessary, in order to make some allowance for delay if any occurred. Weather intensely cold. Not a word spoken. No sound but the dull tramp of the horses through the snow. Marched without hindrance until 3 o'clock a.m., when column halted and was ordered to dismount. Supposed to be as near the Indians as we dare approach until daylight. No Indian fires to be seen. Cold increasing. Men actually freezing.

"Not daring to approach nearer the watchful enemy, for fear of alarming him before we could see to properly dispose of him; and the cold steadily gaining in its effects upon the men; it became painfully certain that something must be done, to keep human blood in condition for a boil—the time for which was so near at hand. The men made circles about the size of circus rings, and ran in them to keep warm. It was a curious scene, in the center of that snowy desert, a company of 80 men, on that terrible night, running around in circles as if running for their lives. All running—Captain, Piutes, and all and this performance continued actively for 3 long hours. Even with this extraordinary effort to save themselves, over 20 men were frozen—their hands, feet, or faces. Notwithstanding all they suffered, not a murmur of complaint was uttered by the soldiers. The horses huddled up close together, and were covered with a white mantle of frost; seeming frozen together.

"Daylight came. The intense cold aroused the Indians early, and immediately after daylight fires arose about 5 miles west of the command—although it did not appear near so far. All was excitement in a moment. Capt. Conrad, cool and

deliberate under all circumstances, ordered the men to carefully examine their fire arms, adjust and secure their saddles
properly, and prepare for action. He then divided the command into three columns—Lieut. Duncan, Co. I, commanding
right column, Sergeant Korble, Co. B, commanding the left,
and Conrad the center. The columns took their respective
positions, and advanced—with intervals of three quarters of a
mile between columns, until near the Indians, when each column was ordered into line and the fight commenced in all
its fury. The Indian encampments were on the western side
of Fish creek Valley, about 60 miles west of Paradise Valley—
the mountains of the west forming a half-circle around the
camps, about $3\frac{1}{2}$ miles distant. The Indians had the advantage of the ground. The field fought over was about 2 miles
square, and a large portion of it was covered with tules, and
tall rye grass, and very much cut up with gullies and ravines;
and bore also a great quantity of Spanish broom. The Indians
could not have selected a field better adapted to their style
of warfare. The Indians discovered the three columns dash-
ing down on them when about a mile distant, and then they
could be distinctly seen preparing for battle: dividing off into
squads of from 4 to 6, and selecting their places for combat
where it would be most difficult to maneuver cavalry. Each
warrior had from 50 to 75 poisoned arrows, giving each squad
from 250 to 350 shots. The moment before the battle commenced, owing to the extreme cold a dense cloud of frost commenced flying, so thick that a horseman could not be distinctly
seen over 100 yards. This gave the Indians a great advantage,
as it compelled the soldiers to fight at short range, so that the
bow and arrow could be used; and it also increased the chances
of escape for the Indians. Had the frost commenced flying
earlier, no doubt many of them would have escaped. The
plan of battle was such that the right and left columns flanked
the Indians, and soon surrounded them. They fought with
desperation. In no instance did a warrior lay down his arms
till he laid down his life. They arranged their arrows between
their fingers in such a manner that they could shoot them very
rapidly, and charged with as much bravery as any soldiers in

the world. The excitement was intense. Soldiers, citizens, and the savages, charging and yelling; each straining all his powers to destroy the other; the wild, ringing war-whoop; the rapid firing of 80 disciplined men; the thunder of a cavalry charge; all, together, created a scene that beggars description. Capt. Conrad seemed everywhere in the fight—now leading his men in a charge, now fighting single-handed; and no peril did he not share with his men—never asking them to go where he would not lead. Lieut. Duncan behaved nobly, and is a brave and gallant soldier. Sergeant Korble led his column into the action in the most gallant manner, striking the enemy the first blow, and continuing to fight nobly throughout the battle.

"Dr. Snow, a citizen physician accompanying the detachment from Company I, will be long remembered and loved by the gallant men who fought that day. He rode over all parts of the field during the battle, attending to the wounded soldiers where they fell, applying the antidotes necessary to destroy the deadly effect produced by poisoned arrows—which if not attended to at once must prove fatal. An old man, whose head is white with the frost of many Winters, but whose heart is as warm and his energies as vigorous as those of a youth, he braved the perils of frost and battle to alleviate the suffering of his fellow man. May God protect him, is the soldier's prayer. Many heroic deeds were performed. Each individual was a hero, and none but faced death like veterans. . . .

"The battle, with the exception of a few straggling shots, was over. The Indians had fought with a heroism that astonished everyone who witnessed it. They made no offer to surrender; uttered no sound but yells of defiance; and continued to fire their poisoned arrows until they were so weak that they could throw them but a few feet; and some of them dying would shoot an arrow stright up in the air, in hope that the deady missile would fall on the heated and victorious foe. At the close of the battle 35 dead Indians lay on the field with their bows and quivers still clutched in their hands. All were large, powerful men—a picked company of braves, prepared for battle. But 5 squaws were in the band, and they were acting in the capacity of pack train. Two of these were killed in battle by mistake; the other three were furnished with some provisions and left unmolested.

"Scouting parties made the entire circuit of the field, and found that no living thing had escaped, as the snow was 3 inches deep and there were no tracks leading from the camp. . . .

"The Indian camps all destroyed, the wounded all cared for, the command marched for Fish creek, where water could be obtained, and camped—the trains having arrived there before them. On the night of the 12th snow fell, and the morning of the 13th was blustering and stormy. At daylight marched for Cane Springs. After the command had started, and as the last of the pack train was leaving camp, they saw an Indian coming on the trail from the direction of the battle field. They awaited his arrival, and he proved to be an Indian lad of about 15 years, who had determined to join the whites and was ready to be reconstructed. The Captain was summoned from the front, and with the aid of the interpreters the boy made the following statement: He said that an old man, a young man and himself, were in the mountains the morning of the battle, and knew nothing of it until in the afternoon, when they came down to the camp. He said all the fighting men engaged in the battle were dead but 4, 3 of them being mortally wounded and the other shot through the legs. These 4 wounded men he found hidden in the tules and rye grass. He says that there are no other Indians in those mountains at this time, except those that were with him the morning of the battle. Wounded all comfortable cared for and put in wagons, and the command reached Cane Springs on the night of the 13th. Willow Point Station, in Paradise Valley the night of the 14th, and Dun Glen in the afternoon of the 15th; having made the ride from Willow Point Station to Dun Glen, 47 miles, in 7 hours."

Other smaller engagements occurred during the next several years, but the Fish Creek Valley fight was the last of the large battles of the northern desert.

It is impossible to judge accurately whether or not the Win-

nemucca Lake and Granite Creek Station events were responsible for the beginning of the 1865-66 conflict; but in his half-
century-old history, A. M. Fairchild relates, "A man who once
lived in this valley told that in the early days he met an Indian who had a good rifle. After some talk he bought the gun
and paid the Indian for it. He went on a short distance, and
then returned and followed the Indian and shot him. He took
from his dead body the money he had paid for the gun and
went his way rejoicing; thinking, no doubt, that it was a good
joke on the Indian, and that he had done some clever financial work . . . it will be seen that in many cases, before a massacre by the Indians took place, one or more Indians had been
killed for the fun of it. . . ."

Much of the complete story of the Indian war of 1865 undoubtedly has been lost along with many other non-recorded
memories of the past. But the information contained in the
old newspapers and other documents is sufficient to determine
that the warriors of the Black Rock deserve mention in any
history of the Nevada desert.

CHAPTER IV

The Mohave Desert

IT HAS A spectacular beauty—great, jagged mountains of banded limestone rising high above desert valleys; vast basins sparsely dotted with the green of the creosote bush and the silvery tint of the burrobush on the gray, desert soil; dry stream beds; Joshua trees; dunes of white sand; and endless, sunbright space. To some it is austere and frightening; to others it has a lonely grandeur which is friendly and comforting.

It can be unbearably hot or unpleasantly cold, but during many months of the year its climate is comfortable and healthy. To its thousands of visitors it offers an exciting change of environment, and their numbers are increasing each year.

Because most highway maps label only the California portion of the Mohave (also spelled Mojave) Desert, many travelers consider it limited to the confines of that state. Actually it stretches into four states. Small portions lap over into the southwestern corner of Utah and into northwestern Arizona, and the remainder is divided between Nevada and California. Most of the Mohave lies within the boundaries of the Great Basin.

Thousands of years ago it was not an arid land. Rainfall was abundant so that lakes covered many valleys, rivers flowed long distances, and the environment supported such animals as the mammoth, camel, bison, horse, and giant ground sloth. The date of man's first arrival in the region has long been a subject of speculation.

In 1933, in an area called Tule Springs, located about ten miles north of Las Vegas, a scientist found charcoal associated with bones of extinct camels, horses, and bison; and imbedded with this was an obsidian flake which undoubtedly had been made by man. Later that same year another archeologist visited the site and while excavating similar deposits, found two bone objects which he considered to be man-made artifacts. In 1954, when organic material from each of these excavation sites was subjected to radiocarbon 14 dating, it provided a date in excess of 23,800 years before the present. In 1955 and 1956, additional test explorations of the area were carried on, and a radiocarbon 14 sample from a locality where a stone scraper was found, produced a date of more than 28,000 years old.

In February of 1962, a group of prominent scientists agreed that the Tule Springs site should be extensively excavated to determine if man and Pleistocene animals had lived there contemporaneously. Dr. Richard Shutler, Jr., of the Nevada State Museum, was appointed director of the cooperative project.[1]

Bone beds were buried from one to twenty feet by sediments deposited over several hundred centuries, and heavy earthmoving equipment was required to take off the overburden and cut a total of about two miles of trenches twelve feet wide and up to thirty feet deep. Giant bulldozers and motor scrapers, working alongside such dainty archeology tools as dental picks and paint brushes, shaved a delicate few inches of the hard earth at a time, and produced sheer walls along the trenches which provided the scientists with a cross section of the sediments and the story each had to tell about the plants, animals, climatic changes, and geologic history of the area.

A bone tool, thought to be a product of human workmanship; a caliche object, believed to be a bead; and a scraper and five flakes came from deposits dated from 10,000 to 12,000 years before the present. Although bones of extinct animals were found in sediments more than 40,000 years old, no evidence to support the former belief that man had lived there approximately 30,000 years ago was obtained.

After four and one half months of work, during which about 200,000 tons of earth were moved, it was concluded that man

---

1. *Pleistocene Studies in Southern Nevada*, Nevada State Museum, Anthropological Papers Number 13, Carson, City, Nevada, 1967.

Courtesy Adrian Atwater
GREAT, JAGGED MOUNTAINS OF BANDED LIMESTONE RISE HIGH ABOVE DESERT VALLEYS

Courtesy Nevada State Highway Department
THE MOHAVE DESERT IS THE HOME OF THE JOSHUA TREE

A BULLDOZER CUTS A TRENCH ALONG THE TULE SPRINGS WASH

THE SHEER WALLS OF THE TRENCH ALLOW STUDY OF THOUSANDS OF YEARS OF
DEPOSITS AT TULE SPRINGS.

SCIENTISTS EXCAVATE A PILE OF BISON AND CAMEL BONES AT TULE SPRINGS

THE MOST ABUNDANT ANIMAL BONES AT THE TULE SPRINGS WERE THOSE OF AN
EXTINCT SPECIES OF THE CAMEL FAMILY.

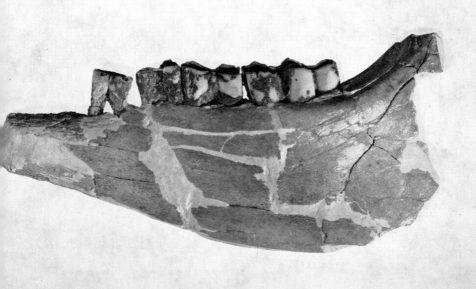

probably came to the area between 11,000 and 13,000 years ago.

The Mohave Desert is rich in archeology sites, many of which probably remain undiscovered. Before being covered by the waters of Lake Mead, the famous Lost City (Pueblo Grande de Nevada) [2] was explored. It is believed to have been built by people related to the Anasazi of northern Arizona and the "four-corner" region of New Mexico, Utah, Colorado, and Arizona.

Beginning about 300 B.C. these Indians lived in round, deep pit houses along the lower stretch of the muddy river—where they made baskets, hunted with dart-throwing atlatls, and gathered seeds and other plant foods. Between A.D. 500 and 700, it is thought they started gathering together in small villages, made pottery, and began growing corn and squash on river-bottom lands.

Their highest development in the area, named the Lost City Phase, apparently occurred between A.D. 700 and 1100, when populations of the villages increased enormously and the people began living not only in pit houses but in adobe and stone surface pueblos, some of which had over a hundred rooms. During this period they were mining salt and turquoise and raising corn, beans, squash, and cotton in fields which were probably irrigated by brush dams and ditches.

And then during the short period between A.D. 1100 and 1150, the Lost City civilization faded away. The villages were moved from near the river to high ridges, perhaps for better defense, and then finally abandoned. The region was taken over by the Southern Paiute people who, in turn, relinquished most of it to the white man about seven hundred years later.

The white man's conquest of the Mohave Desert in many respects parallels that of Nevada's northern desert. The trapper-explorers came first and were soon followed by the travelers who, for one reason or another, desired to reach California. And the stories of the hardships and hazards of the

---

2. *Lost City, Pueblo Grande De Nevada*, Richard Shutler, Jr., Nevada State Museum, Anthropological Papers Number 5, Carson City, Nevada, 1961.

PUEBLO GRANDE DE NEVADA AT SUNRISE

ROOM OUTLINES OF LOST CITY SURFACE DWELLINGS AS THEY APPEAR AFTER TWO
INUNDATIONS BY THE WATERS OF LAKE MEAD.

northern emigrant trail are matched by the exciting journals of adventure along the famed Old Spanish Trail.

Although sections of it had been established earlier, the general route of the entire Spanish Trail is believed to have been first traversed in 1830-31 by the Wolfskill, Yount party of about twenty men. Starting at Santa Fe, New Mexico, the trail made a long loop up into Colorado and Utah to avoid the Grand Canyon and Arizona desert and then turned southwest to enter Nevada near the present towns of Mesquite and Bunkerville. From there it continued to Las Vegas and Mountain Springs before crossing over into California and eventually reaching Los Angeles. It was a rugged twelve-hundred-mile trip over mountains and deserts, but for a number of years it served as a route for the trade of New Mexican blankets and other woolen fabrics for California mules and goods. As protection against Indians and other dangers, most traders traveled in caravans which, on arriving in Los Angeles, scattered to visit other communities to the north and the south. After disposing of their trade goods and acquiring the materials they wished to carry back to Santa Fe, the traders rendezvoused at Los Angeles before beginning the long return journey.

In April of 1844, John Charles Frémont intersected the Old Spanish Trail north of El Cajon Pass in the California portion of the Mohave Desert. He was on the homeward leg of an extraordinary expedition which had begun in Kansas City almost one year before and had taken his party in a great circuitous route to the Great Salt Lake, up to the Columbia River, down through northwestern Nevada, over the Sierras to Sacramento, and now to southern California. One purpose of the journey was to search for the legendary San Buenaventura River which was believed to flow from the Rocky Mountains to San Francisco Bay. Because of his writing ability, Frémont's journal is one of the most interesting and descriptive accounts of early travel over the Spanish Trail.

On April 20, he wrote, "a general shout announced that we had struck the great object of our search—THE SPANISH TRAIL—which here was running directly north. The road itself, and its course, were equally happy discoveries to us. Since the middle of December we had continually been forced south by mountains and by deserts, and now would have to make six degrees of *northing*, to regain the latitude on which we wished to cross the Rocky Mountains. The course of the road, therefore, was what we wanted; and, once more, we felt like going homewards. A *road* to travel on, and the *right* course to go, were joyful consolations to us; and our animals enjoyed the beaten track like ourselves. Relieved from the rocks and brush, our wild mules started off at a rapid rate, and in 15 miles we reached a considerable river, timbered with cottonwood and willow, where we found a bottom of tolerable grass. As the animals had suffered a great deal in the last few days, I remained here all next day, to allow them the necessary repose; and it was now necessary, at every favorable place, to make a little halt. Between us and the Colorado river we were aware that the country was extremely poor in grass, and scarce for water, there being many *jornadas*, (days' journey,) or long stretches of 40 to 60 miles, without water, where the road was marked by bones of animals."

During the next three days, Frémont's party traveled along the stream, which he named the "Mohave river," to a point where, except for a few pools of water, it disappeared. It was on the afternoon of April 24 that two Mexicans, a man named Fuentes and a boy, Pablo, rode into camp to report that their group of six persons—which included Fuentes' wife, Pablo's father and mother, and another man from New Mexico—had been attacked by a band of about one hundred Indians at a place approximately eighty miles farther along the road. The man and boy had escaped with their herd of thirty horses, which they had left at a spring about twenty-five miles distant.

The next morning, accompanied by the two Mexicans, Frémont's company continued along the trail to the spring where the horses had been abandoned. The animals were not in the area, and an examination of the ground indicated that they had been driven off by Indians. Frémont's famous guide, Kit Carson, and a man named Godey, volunteered to accompany

Fuentes in pursuit of the raiders; and following the tracks of the horses, the three men set out. During the evening, Fuentes returned, his horse having given out. Frémont's journal of April 26 reads like fiction.

"In the afternoon of the next day, a war-whoop was heard, such as Indians make when returning from a victorious enterprise; and soon Carson and Godey appeared, driving before them a band of horses, recognised by Fuentes to be part of those they had lost. Two bloody scalps, dangling from the end of Godey's gun, announced that they had overtaken the Indians as well as the horses. They informed us, that after Fuentes left them, from the failure of his horse, they continued the pursuit alone, and towards nightfall entered the mountains, into which the trail led. After sunset the moon gave light, and they followed the trail by moonshine until late in the night, when it entered a narrow defile, they tied up their horses, struck no fire, and lay down to sleep in silence and in darkness. Here they lay from midnight till morning. At daylight they resumed the pursuit, and about sunrise discovered the horses; and, immediately dismounting and tying up their own, they crept cautiously to a rising ground which intervened, from the crest of which they perceived the encampment of four lodges close by. They proceeded quietly, and had got within thirty or forty yards of their object, when a movement among the horses discovered them to the Indians; giving the war shout, they instantly charged into the camp, regardless of the number which the *four* lodges would imply. The Indians received them with a flight of arrows shot from their long bows, one of which passed through Godey's shirt collar, barely missing the neck; our men fired their rifles upon a steady aim, and rushed in. Two Indians were stretched on the ground, fatally pierced with bullets; the rest fled, except a lad that was captured. The scalps of the fallen were instantly stripped off; but in the process, one of them, who had two balls through his body, sprung to his feet, the blood streaming from his skinned head, and uttering a hideous howl. An old squaw, possibly his mother, stopped and looked back from the mountain side she was climbing, threatening and lamenting. The frightful spectacle appalled the stout hearts of our men; but they did what humanity required, and quickly terminated the agonies of the gory savage. They were now masters of the camp, which was a pretty little recess in the mountains, with a fine spring, and apparently safe from all invasion. Great preparations had been made to feast a large party, for it was a very proper place for a rendezvous, and for the celebration of such orgies as robbers of the desert would delight in. Several of the best horses had been killed, skinned, and cut up; for the Indians living in the mountains, and only coming into the plains to rob and murder, make no other use of horses than to eat them. Large earthen vessels were on the fire, boiling and stewing the horse beef; and several baskets, containing fifty or sixty pairs of moccasins, indicated the presence, or expectation, of a considerable party. They released the boy, who had given strong evidence of the stoicism, or something else, of the savage character, in commencing his breakfast upon a horse's head as soon as he found he was not to be killed, but only tied as a prisoner. Their object accomplished, our men gathered up all surviving horses, fifteen in number, returned upon their trail, and rejoined us at our camp in the afternoon of the same day. They had rode about one hundred miles in pursuit and return, and all in thirty hours. The time, place, object, and numbers, considered, this expedition of Carson and Godey may be considered among the boldest and most disinterested which the annals of western adventure, so full of daring deeds, can present. Two men, in a savage desert, pursue day and night an unknown body of Indians into the defiles of an unknown mountain—attack them on sight, without counting numbers—and defeat them in an instant—and for what? To punish the robbers of the desert, and to avenge the wrongs of Mexicans whom they did not know. I repeat: it was Carson and Godey who did this—the former an *American*, born in the Boonslick county of Missouri; the latter a Frenchman, born in St. Louis—and both trained to western enterprise from early life."

When, several days later, Frémont reached the place where the Mexicans had been first attacked, he found the mutilated bodies of two men; but the two women were missing—apparently taken captive.

The trail soon crossed into Nevada and on May 3, Frémont wrote, "After a day's journey of 18 miles, in a northeasterly direction, we encamped in the midst of another very large basin, at a camping ground called *las Vegas*—a term which the Spaniards used to signify fertile or marshy plains, in contradistinction to *llanos,* which they apply to dry and sterile plains. Two narrow streams of clear water, four to five feet deep, gush suddenly, with a quick current, from two singularly large springs; these, and other waters of the basin, pass out in a gap to the eastward. The taste of the water is good, but rather too warm to be agreeable; the temperature being 71° in the one, and 73° in the other. They, however, afforded a delightful bathing place."

Early the next morning, the company started the trek across the most forbidding section of the Old Spanish Trail—the waterless area between Las Vegas and the present-day town of Moapa and the Muddy River. Passing many skeletons of horses along the road, Frémont mentioned the oppressive heat and the intolerable thirst while traveling over "hot, yellow sands."

Hoping to find water, the party kept pushing on for sixteen hours until, about midnight, the mules smelled water and began running; and soon they came to "a bold, running stream."

Because of the exhausted condition of his animals, Frémont decided to camp and rest at the Muddy River during the following day. However, according to his journal, the pause offered little relaxation for his men.

"Indians crowded numerously around us in the morning and we were obliged to keep arms in hand all day, to keep them out of the camp. They began to surround the horses, which, for the convenience of grass, we were guarding a little above, on the river. These were immediately driven in, and kept close to the camp.

"In the darkness of the night we had made a very bad encampment, our fires being commanded by a rocky bluff within 50 yards; but, notwithstanding, we had the river and small thickets of willows on the other side. Several times during the day the camp was insulted by the Indians; but, peace being our object, I kept simply on the defensive. Some of the Indians were scattered in every direction over the hills. Their language being probably a dialect of the *Utah,* with the aid of signs some of our people could comprehend them very well. They were the same people who had murdered the Mexicans; and towards us their disposition was evidently hostile, nor were we well disposed towards them. They were barefooted, and nearly naked; their hair gathered up into a knot behind; and with his bow, each man carried a quiver with thirty or forty arrows partially drawn out. Besides these, each held in his hand two or three arrows for instant service. Their arrows are barbed with a very clear translucent stone, a species of opal, nearly as hard as the diamond; and, shot from their long bow, are almost as effective as a gunshot.

"A man who appeared to be a chief, with two or three others, forced himself into camp, bringing with him his arms, in spite of my orders to the contrary. When shown our weapons, he bored his ear with his fingers, and said he could not hear. 'Why,' said he, 'there are none of you.' Counting the people around the camp, and including in the number a mule which was being shod, he made out 22. 'So many,' said he, showing the number, 'and we—we are a great many'; and he pointed to the hills and mountains round about. 'If you have your arms,' said he, twanging his bow, 'we have these.' I had some difficulty in restraining the people, particularly Carson, who felt an insult of this kind as much as if it had been given by a more responsible being. 'Don't say that, old man,' said he; 'don't you say that—your life's in danger'—speaking in good English; and probably the old man was nearer his end than he will be before he meets it."

After losing several animals to the Indians, the company set out again the next morning for a twenty-mile march to the

Virgin River. With Indians stealthily following them, "like a band of wolves," they traveled up this stream to cross into Arizona. On May 9, while searching for a lame mule, a man named Tabeau was killed by the Indians.

On May 17, Frémont left the Old Spanish Trail, which now turned to the southeast, and set a course for Utah Lake—arriving there seven days later. The great circular journey of the Far West had been completed, and it had proved that the legendary San Buenaventura waterway did not exist.

But of greater importance, the expedition brought a realization that a vast area lying between the Wasatch range of Utah and the Sierra Nevadas was a land of interior drainage. The names Frémont gave to the places he explored were often descriptive—and so he called this region "the Great Basin."

During the years that followed, the Old Spanish Trail continued to make history—the forty-niners who followed it en route to California gold fields, the Mormons who established a mission and fort at Las Vegas—but few would write as dramatically or descriptively as Frémont of their adventures along it across the Mohave Desert.

CHAPTER V

Memories of the Desert's
Gold Seekers

THE FORTY-NINERS, intent on reaching California gold camps, fought their way across the Nevada desert and in their hurry passed by more than one of nature's great storehouses of precious metals. It was not until the next decade that the main door to the famous Comstock treasure was opened, and such names as Eldorado Canyon, Pioche, Unionville, Eureka, Austin, Belmont, Hamilton, and Tuscarora became known to the mining world.[1]

Fortunes were made and lost in the early camps; but during the last quarter of the eighteen hundreds their productivity declined so that many of their inhabitants, believing that the desert's wealth was exhausted, moved to newer discoveries in Alaska and even South Africa.

And then on a spring day of the first year of the new century, in an area which native Indians called "Tonopah," James L. Butler found a piece of vein quartz rich in silver and gold. The boom was on again; and it was intensified when, thirty miles to the south of Tonopah, another rich discovery exploded the small camp of Goldfield into Nevada's largest city. Other camps such as Rhyolite, Manhattan, Round Mountain, Rawhide, Wonder, Silver Peak, Ramsey, and Fairview were being staked out in isolated areas of both the Mohave and Great Basin deserts, and large beds of copper ore were being exposed in the eastern section of the state.

The rich silver ore of the Comstock, Tonopah, and other Nevada mines provided most of the state's early mineral

---

1. According to F. C. Lincoln, "Aside from the early mines of the Indians and of the Franciscan monks, the Potosi Mine in the Yellow Pine Mining District is the oldest *lode* mine in Nevada. It was discovered by a party of Mormons returning . . . over the old Spanish Trail in 1855." The Potosi mine lies southwest of Las Vegas.

wealth. But perhaps to most humans gold is the most fascinating of all the precious metals, and when the incredibly high-grade ore of Goldfield began coming from the ground, it attracted men from around the world.

Many stories about Goldfield—its discovery, its great boom —have been written. But from people who experienced those exciting days there still remain a few memories which are unrecorded. Claude Lund's story is an example.

"During the fall of 1888, itinerant construction workers traveled on foot from Frisco, Utah, through Snake Valley, Nevada, en route to the hydraulic operations at the placer mining camp of Oseaolo. Sixty of the eighty-mile trip was desert, and some of the tired men stopped at our Snake Valley ranch to spend the night. One of them was named Tom Notes.

"Notes was a large, handsome man of about forty-five who hoped to someday be a rancher. Because of this interest, my father offered him a job; and during the following months Notes developed into an efficient ranch hand.

"To a five-year-old boy, he soon became a hero. He bought me candy, told me stories, and called me his partner. He singled me out from my five brothers and, to me, there was no better man in all Nevada.

"During the winter of 1888, Tom somehow obtained information that a certain 160 acres of land, lying near the center of a large ranch holding, was open to homesteading. In those days legal descriptions and fencing of large ranches were faulty, and land within their boundaries was sometimes unclaimed. The Utah-Nevada state line bisected Snake Valley and Tom proved his finding in the Millard County, Utah, courthouse. He then homesteaded the quarter section of rich land.

"He was starting to build his log cabin and barn when the owners of the surrounding ranch made their first offer to purchase the property. His refusal to sell brought threats, which increased in their seriousness during the following months.

"It was in the summer of 1889 that Tom Notes was mur-

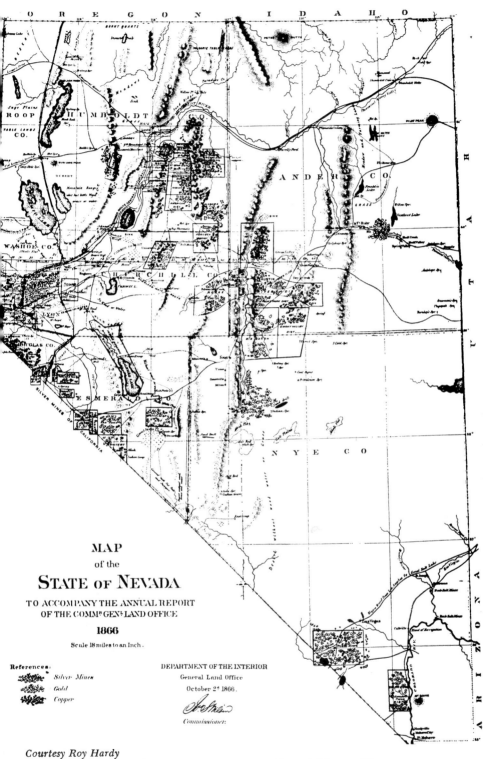

An Interesting, if Inaccurate, 1866 Map of the Desert's Mineral Wealth

dered. He was found lying between his new house and barn; he had been shot in the back.

"Authorities were far away, transportation was slow, and it was three days before a sheriff's posse arrived. There were no clues, but on the strength of their threats, the owners of the surrounding ranch were arrested and brought to trial in Millard County. Because of insufficient evidence they were acquitted, and eventually the case was forgotten—forgotten by everyone except me, a six-year-old kid who swore that some-day he would find the murderer of his partner.

"To give my brothers and me proper schooling, my father moved to Utah. Years later, I returned to northern Nevada to work as a cowpuncher.

"It was in April, 1903, that I got the mining fever and headed for Tonopah. In August of that year, I left Tonopah on a prospecting trip to the unorganized mining district called "Grandpah," later to be named Goldfield, and during the following spring located claims there on land which eventually became a part of the city.

"During the winter of 1904, there were three saloons, one grocery store, and two feedlots in the town. Johnnie Jones, Bert Higgins, and Bob Martin owned the Gold Wedge saloon which consisted of a tent about twenty feet long and fourteen feet wide, framed and floored with pine. There was little money in circulation in the camp, but we could get whiskey on credit at the Gold Wedge bar, and there was heat from a big stove in the center of the tent where we played cards—providing there was enough wood to keep the stove hot.

"Wood was supplied to the town by a grizzled old Frenchman called Jerry. A booze-fighter, he earned his whiskey money hauling piñon and juniper logs to the camp on a battered freight wagon pulled by two ancient crowbait horses. The wood supply was uncertain, depending on whether Jerry had recovered from the alcohol that money or credit always bought.

"However, of more concern to us than the uncertainty of our wood supply was Jerry's neglect of his horses. A horse or a mule was a valuable asset to a desert mining camp—some-

SOME OF RHYOLITE'S OLD STONE WALLS STILL STAND

GOLDFIELD IN 1903, WHEN CLAUDE LUND FIRST ARRIVED THERE

thing on which a man's life might depend. Although we were a rough bunch, we took care of our animals and they were fed before a man looked to his own meal. And so when two half starved horses stood unharnessed night after night, the population of Goldfield became concerned.

"Reprimands and warnings were given the old drunk, but they had no effect. Finally a group of us decided to hold a kangaroo court, a mock trial to attempt to scare old Jerry into taking better care of his horses.

"Plans were made around the stove on a cold winter night. I was chosen to act as sheriff, an ex-lawyer was selected as District Attorney, and a hard-rock miner, who knew something about legal procedures, was appointed judge. A jury was formed from the rest of the men, and we planned the trial carefully.

"On the night of February eighteenth, during a heavy snowstorm, I located Jerry in another bar and arrested him. Court was called to order in the saloon, where the prisoner, confused and unsteady with alcohol, was pushed into a chair. Above him a hangman's noose hung from a crossbeam.

"Witnesses were called who testified as to the drunkard's treatment of his horses. There was no defense attorney, and Jerry did not deny the accusations. The District Attorney made a dramatic summary; the judge notified the prisoner that if the jury returned a verdict of guilty, he would be hung by the neck until dead; and the jury was charged. Minutes later the six men returned; their verdict was guilty.

"The judge turned to the prisoner and said, 'You have been found guilty of cruelty to animals in the desert. You will, therefore, be hung immediately. If you have anything on your conscience that you want to confess before you die, now is the time.'

"I was standing in the back of the room watching the old Frenchman's face. Under the light of the kerosene lamps, I could see the sweat on the sides of his thin, wrinkled cheeks. The trial seemed to be having the desired effect but, for a moment, I felt sorry for him. Suddenly tears began running down his face and his voice in broken English came across the room.

"Then, hardly believing what I heard, I listened to a confession of a murder committed sixteen years before—the killing of my friend, Tom Notes.

"Time weakens desire for revenge; and, as the broken old man finished his confession and sat hunched and frightened in his chair, I kept my silence. Such matters as murder were not uncommon in those days, and when Jerry promised to take better care of his horses, he was released.

"He kept that promise for the next seven months—until he was found dead from too much whiskey and exposure. I guess he paid for his crime. I like to remember his trial as desert justice."

Among Nevada mining men, Roy A. Hardy, of Reno, is considered the dean of the state's mining engineers. Born in South Dakota in 1886, Roy's childhood was spent largely in the mining camps of Cripple Creek and Leadville, Colorado. In 1905 he traveled to Tonopah where he was hired by a mining company to investigate various new mineral discoveries over a large area of southern Nevada, southeastern California, and western Utah. Furnished with a buckboard, horse, and a barrel of water, during the next year Roy journeyed from one prospect to another collecting samples of ore which would later be assayed to determine values and potentials.

Following the advice of mining men with whom he was associated, in 1908 he enrolled in the Mackay School of Mines at the University of Nevada where he studied mining engineering, played Rugby football, and at a junior prom, met his future wife, Bonnie Thoma.

Roy's formal mining career began as a geologist at Fairview, Nevada, and during the next half century, led him to such positions as superintendent, general manager, and, in some instances, owner of some of the major gold and silver mines in Nevada. His work took him to many of the mineral districts of the West, but when he talks about his experiences,

he most often goes back to the boom days of Tonopah and
Goldfield. To a young man of nineteen years of age they
were exciting towns.

Roy remembers "Thousands of people—miners, merchants,
gamblers, speculators, and promoters—came there from
around the world, and there were well-known names among
them. For instance, there was Johnny Poe, reputed to be a
relative of Edgar Allen Poe. Johnny was a gambler and when
someone questioned him about the whereabouts of his lug-
gage, Johnny said that he had it with him and that it consisted
of fifty-two pieces—a deck of cards. One time in a Rhyolite
saloon one of the customers ripped an American flag from the
wall. This made Johnny angry—to an extent that by the time
he got through with the man the saloon was a wreck.

"There were many adventurers like Johnny Poe. Tex
Rickard came to Goldfield after taking a try at the Alaskan
Klondike gold rush. He became part owner of Goldfield's
Northern Saloon and helped to organize the Goldfield Athletic
Association which brought the world lightweight champion-
ship fight between champion Joe Gans and challenger Battling
Nelson to Goldfield in 1906. This fight may have given Rick-
ard the experience which allowed him in later years to operate
New York's Madison Square Garden.

"There were nationally prominent people like Charles
Schwab, owner of Bethlehem Steel, and United States Senators
Key Pittman, Tasker Oddie, and the incomparable William
M. Stewart. Stewart, who settled in Virginia City in 1860 and
four years later was elected one of Nevada's first United States
Senators, had retired after a total of twenty-nine years in the
Senate and was living in Rhyolite. I remember him as a big
man about six feet three inches tall who weighed over two hundred pounds and had a long, white beard. He was a dynamic
person who took charge of everything and everyone around
him. I lived in a cabin near the small stone office building
in which Stewart was writing his memoirs, and I soon learned
that the Senator had a habit of repeating to himself, in a loud
voice, each sentence that he wrote. So I guess I was one of

DURING TONOPAH'S EARLY DAYS, ITS RESIDENTS DEPENDED ON THESE WAGONS
FOR THEIR WATER.

GOLDFIELD WHEN IT WAS NEVADA'S LARGEST CITY

the first to know parts of the Stewart autobiography—long before it was published.

"I first met George Wingfield in the winter of 1905 in the camp of Manhattan, and this meeting eventually resulted in a friendship and association which lasted for over fifty years.

"When he was twenty-two years old, George drove a trail herd of cattle from Lakeview, Oregon, to Winnemucca; and deciding to remain in Nevada, he worked as a cowhand in the Humboldt river ranching area. Early in 1901 he moved to the new town of Tonopah where he eventually obtained an interest in the gambling concession of the famous Tonopah Club. He began acquiring mine properties and these investments were so successful that in 1906, in partnership with Winnemucca banker George S. Nixon, he was buying and consolidating the mines of the Goldfield district. This resulted in the Goldfield Consolidated Mines Company, one of the nation's largest gold producers.

"George Wingfield was an unusual person in many ways. He was reserved in speech, seldom if ever talked about himself, and disliked publicity. He was a strong man who associated with the roughest inhabitants of a mining camp, but he never used profanity. Following the death of Senator Nixon in 1912, he refused an appointment to the United States Senate.

"He was capable of making lasting friendships. When he was working as a cowboy in the Winnemucca area, he met Herbert Hoover on an ore train traveling between Golconda and the Adelaide mine where Hoover was employed as a mining engineer. This was the start of a friendship between the two men which lasted throughout Wingfield's life. Bernard Baruch was another of his close friends.

"There were many stories about him. I remember the one about the time he won a Tonopah gambling club in a game of cards and then gave most of it back to the loser. It was widely recognized that he always kept his word, and most of his business deals were not made in writing. I understand that when United Airlines moved its office into Wingfield's Riverside hotel in Reno, George refused to sign a written lease prepared by the company's attorneys. The airline's president, William Patterson, flew to Reno to negotiate the matter—with the result that his company became a party to the one lease in its history which was sealed with only a handshake.

"Once George moved to Nevada, he spent the rest of his life here. He did much for the state.

"The high grade ore of the Goldfield mines was some of the richest ever found in this country. Some of it brought over ten thousand dollars a ton, and it was reported that a check for more than a half million dollars was received for one carload.

"The rock was so rich that some of the miners began concealing pieces of it in their pockets or lunch buckets when they left the mines. The ore was then crushed and sold to an assayer who bought it at a price at which he could make a good profit.

"It wasn't long before this 'highgrading' was pretty much of an accepted practice—even to the extent that stores sold specially made shirts and pants with hidden pockets and offered hats with double crowns. One time a miner going off shift fell down. His pockets were so heavy with gold ore he couldn't get up.

"The mine owners were losing many thousands of dollars a month until George Wingfield started a system of change rooms where miners were required to change their outer clothes and leave them in a locker before going off shift. This regulation probably was one of the causes of the labor troubles which later developed.

"By nineteen twenty, the big Goldfield deposits—which in fifteen years had produced more than eighty million dollars —were fairly well mined out. It wasn't long before cloudbursts and fires had left only a few of the city's buildings, standing; and other camps like Rhyolite were almost deserted.

"During the next ten years there were no new spectacular gold or silver discoveries, and this led some people to believe that all of the big deposits had been found.

"In the summer of 1935, George Wingfield and Noble Getchell asked me to go with them to look at a property about

forty miles east of Winnemucca. When still some distance
away, we stopped the car and they pointed out a large outcrop
of quartz. I remember turning to George and Noble and
saying, 'This is elephant hunting ground—if there's anything
here, it should be big.'

"It had taken quite a few centuries of erosion to wear away
the surrounding softer rock and expose the apex of this quartz
vein which was over two hundred feet wide. Its surface had
been scratched and nicked by prospectors, probably as early
as the eighteen seventies, but when they had panned their
samples they had never found anything of value.

"But in 1934 two prospectors, named Emmet Chase (whom
Getchell had once grubstaked) and Ed Knight, camped in
the gulley below the outcrop and dug into the footwall of the
vein. Unlike the prospectors before them, they had a sample
of the rock fire-assayed, and the report showed a value of two
dollars per ton.

"Chase, a former cowhand who had participated in the last
Nevada Indian fight in 1911, reported his assay to Getchell,
who in turn contacted Wingfield. Although ore running two
dollars to the ton was short of commercial value, when I saw
the size of the vein, I recommended further exploratory work.
George and Noble purchased several sections of the area from
the Central Pacific Railroad, and I hired a crew of three
miners.

"We first dug a crosscut into the hanging wall of the vein
(the side opposite Chase and Knight's prospect) and hit ore
almost immediately. Surprisingly, it assayed eight to twelve
dollars in gold to the ton. We called it 'no see um gold' because the grains were so fine they couldn't be seen when they
were panned. Tunneling in both directions of the vein and
at a lower level, proved the ore body to be both large and con-
sistent in commercial value.

"Well, that was the beginning of the famous Getchell Mine.
Wingfield's long time friend, Bernard Baruch participated in
financing a mill, and by 1940 the mine was the largest gold
producer in Nevada and ranked fifth in importance in the
United States. The mining of tungsten began on the prop-

THE GIANT QUARTZ OUTCROP OF THE GETCHELL MINE AFTER WORK HAD BEGUN

THE GETCHELL MINE WHEN IT WAS ONE OF THE NATION'S LARGE PRODUCERS OF
GOLD AND TUNGSTEN.

erty in 1951, and by 1956 the Getchell was believed to be the third largest producer of that metal in the nation."

Roy Hardy is still following his profession. He is currently president of three Nevada mining companies and is secretary and engineer of Mines Exploration Incorporated which is doing work at Red Mountain in California's section of the Mohave Desert.

Pointing out the new Carlin Mine in north central Nevada, which in the last several years has become one of the three top gold producers in the nation, Roy is confident that bonanzas still remain to be found in the Nevada desert.

He has been searching for them for over sixty years—and if you ask him he will tell you, "It's been a damned good life."

CHAPTER VI

Desert Grass and the Big Spread

TO TIPTON LINDSEY, urging his tired and hungry oxen along the trail to California, the desert's grass was as essential as its water and, for the past fourteen days, more difficult to obtain. The thousands of other oxen, mules, and horses which had earlier passed this way had closely cropped the meadowlands bordering the Humboldt River, and the sandy foothills above the road were barren. Time did not allow a more distant search for forage, for ahead, beyond the desert, lay the Sierra Nevada whose summit must be crossed before storms closed its passes. Under the date of August 10, 1849, Lindsey noted in his diary,[1] "Continued down the valley—had no feed but willows."

To Tipton Lindsey, the country through which he traveled was "one of sterile desolation."

But beyond the sight and reach of the weary emigrants on the Humboldt trail there existed vast areas of rangeland untouched by man's domestic animals. Scattered over thousands of square miles and growing beneath and between desert shrubs, nutritious native plants such as Indian ricegrass, wild rye, and wheatgrasses were available for harvest. Along rivers, or where small streams issued from mountain canyons to flow short distances before sinking into valley floors, natural meadows offered sites for ranching headquarters.

It was sheep and cattle country, and a decade after Lindsey's journey, livestock men began trailing their herds to its open range. By the late 1870's, more than 200,000 cattle and

---

1. Tipton Lindsey, "The Plains and Deserts of North America, A Journal of a Trip to California (Overland)," 1849, Autograph Manuscript Signed, Bancroft Library, University of California.

200,000 sheep are estimated to have been grazing Nevada's high desert.

But by this time certain large areas of the ranges were becoming overstocked, and this combined with periodic drouth had injured the grasses and browse. The winter of 1879-80 was exceptionally severe, and the deep snows and low temperatures brought heavy livestock losses. During 1880 many discouraged ranchers moved to other states, to be soon replaced by hardy newcomers. It was during the next half century that the great livestock empires were built, and sometimes lost, in the Nevada desert.

Some of the empire builders, through the stories handed down, have become legendary. Henry Miller, of the vast Miller and Lux outfit; John Sparks, who built one of Elko County's large cattle holdings and also served the state as governor; Pedro Altube and the famous Spanish ranch; W. H. "Bill" Moffatt, whose attempt with Herbert J. Humphrey to corner the United States wool market resulted in bankruptcy but who rebuilt to develop the Moffatt "Manteca-fed Beef"; L. R. "Broadhorns" Bradley; Pat Flanigan; W. T. Jenkins, Warren W. Williams and many others are names which are remembered—the men who built the great ranches.

Did it take a certain kind of person to compete successfully with the harsh environment of the Great Basin? Those who succeeded were a small percentage of those who tried. What type of man was able to acquire and rule a vast domain of desert rangelands?

* * *

On Tuesday, May 27, 1941, many Nevada newspapers featured two headline stories. One dealt with the sinking, by Great Britain's naval forces, of the prized German battleship, *Bismarck*. The other announced the death of John G. Taylor, "a man who forged one of the greatest livestock empires known to the west."

The Winnemucca, Nevada, *Humboldt Star* newspaper reported in part:

"The stockman who started his climb up the path to more than a millionaire by herding sheep in northern Nevada died between 12:00 and 1:00 o'clock yesterday afternoon at his Hot Springs ranch, 50 miles east of Winnemucca in Humboldt county—a property he saved when the depression took his lands from him. . . .

"Ill for the past month with a heart ailment, an attack is believed to have brought death to this friend of United States senators and herders alike. . . .

"VAST EMPIRE

"Familiarly known as 'John G.' to his countless friends, Taylor's lands once stretched so far it is told that his sheep or cattle could be driven from Lovelock to well up into Idaho without their setting foot on anything but Taylor holdings. His holdings . . . once contained 60,000 head of sheep, 8,000 cattle and 800 blooded horses and numbered more than 130,000 acres of land, more than 500,000 acres of leased land and thousands upon thousands of acres of public domain he occupied.

Courtesy Nevada Historical Society
THE MILLER AND LUX QUINN RIVER CROSSING RANCH IN 1898

"BORN IN SCOTLAND

"Born at Glasgow, Scotland, on April 30, 1854, to parents of Scotch descent, he came to the United States alone when only a boy of fourteen. John Gilmore Taylor arrived in New York City, went to Texas for a brief time and came West to California. Believed to have settled in California at the town of Lodi first, Taylor went into the employ of the old Miller and Lux Stock company. Leaving the stock business, he went into the employ of O'Conner and Moffat, men's furnishings concern in San Francisco, California, in 1876.

"His employ in the Bay city store was brief and he came to Nevada where stories say he sheared his first sheep at Tacoma, an old sheep-raising area in eastern Nevada. Taylor then began sheep-herding, a career which led him to be a millionaire through taking the hard knocks along the path to success and good fortune. He was said to have been employed by a man named Welch at Taber mountain in the Lovelock area and was seen there by Dan 'Uncle Dan' Wheeler, one of the biggest of stockmen of that time.

"WORKS FOR WHEELER

" 'Uncle Dan' Wheeler was quoted as saying in the early years that he didn't put John G. Taylor into business but that Taylor put himself there. In any event, Taylor went into the employ of Wheeler as a ranch hand on the Lake and Wheeler Home ranches about 1886. The long-remembered hard winter of 1889-1890 brought ruin to most of the Nevada stockmen, but John Taylor emerged on the road to being a millionaire after Taylor had purchased his first ranch property at Rye Patch, Pershing county.

"Stories are told that during the severe winter he worked like a Trojan to save his stock. He chopped down trees, dug up stumps and bushes from beneath the snow and then made huge fires which melted the snow and uncovered forage for his sheep. . . .

"FASHIONS EMPIRE

"From that start, Taylor fashioned his vast empire to be known as John G. Taylor, Inc. Taylor then acquired more ranching properties in Elko, Humboldt and Pershing coun-

JOHN G. TAYLOR, LIVESTOCK EMPIRE BUILDER OF THE NEVADA DESERT

ties including the Upper and Lower Clover, Hot Springs, Thomas Canyon and others in Humboldt county, I. L., Spanish, Columbia, V. N., S. L., and others in Elko county, Rye Patch and many others in the Lovelock area. . . .

"Taylor's Nevada headquarters were maintained at Lovelock and that town served as the hub of perhaps the greatest stock and ranch empire ever built in Nevada and one of the largest in the West."

Other newspaper stories of May 27 contained interesting portrayals of Taylor such as, "one of the most colorful and picturesque stockmen of the old school," and, "never one to heed everyday conventions."

What type of man was John G. Taylor?

"My father," Jeanette Taylor Cloud explains, "was probably an enigma to many of the people who knew him. Undoubtedly he was highly respected—his ability, his manner, his appearance, almost everything about him commanded respect. But certain personal characteristics, his individuality, encouraged the stories—perhaps you might almost call them legends—which were told about him.

"He was about six feet tall and straight as a ruler. He never gained weight; he was always straight and lean. To me he looked the same until the day he died—he didn't age; he didn't change.

"Even in his later years he could outwalk any of his employees and probably most horses. If you walked with him you had to run to keep up.

"In Scotland his formal education was limited, but he was highly self-educated. He did not read trivial fiction but enjoyed biographies, historical novels, poetry, some periodicals, and the Bible. Although he had no formal religion, he approved of other people attending church. His speech had more of a British than Scottish accent; but when he read Robert Burns's poetry to me, he could burr with the best of the Scots.

"My father was never really interested in acquiring money,

and he never desired comforts for himself. I have always believed, and I have heard my mother and others say, that his ambition was not to gain financial wealth per se; but if he could have owned every stick of sagebrush in Nevada, he would have been very happy. He loved the state.

"He really had no hobbies; his ranching business was his life. He had fantastic physical stamina and health; I can remember him being ill only twice. Once he drank water out of a canteen that contained gasoline. Another time he had a strangulated hernia and was rushed to Reno for surgery. On the way the strangulation corrected itself, but he was placed in the hospital to have the hernia surgically repaired the next morning. After seeing to his admittance at St. Mary's Hospital, my mother went to a hotel. The next day she learned that when the nurses had gone to prepare my father for surgery they had found his room empty. During the night he had gotten dressed and taken a train to Winnemucca. He never had the hernia repaired.

"He was the most fastidious man I have ever known. Whether he was out in a sheep camp or anywhere, he was always clean. He hated dust; he despised dirt. His working clothes, while he was on his ranches or at his sheep or cow camps, were rather unusual. He wore bib overalls; but underneath them he had on a pair of good suit pants, a clean and starched white shirt, and a hard and detachable white collar. He always wore the hard white collar; and he often would tie a bandanna around it.

"When he was in San Francisco or another city he was very much the cultured gentleman. He wore expensive suits made for him by a tailor, and a hat something like a homburg.

"He spoke very well, was always very tidy; and with a trimmed mustache had a distinguished appearance.

"My mother and I lived in San Francisco part of each year; we would go there in the late Fall. I would attend school until after Christmas, and then we would return to Nevada where I would go to school for the remainder of the year. We had a house in San Francisco; and when he could, my father would come down with the intention of staying with us for several

weeks. But in a few days he always became nervous from in-
activity and would return to Nevada.

"Regardless of whether he was in San Francisco or Lovelock he always arose early—about 4:00 A.M. He wanted his
breakfast at a terrible hour, and we lost lots of cooks because
of that. One time, at two o'clock in the morning, there was a
fire near our house in Lovelock. Sparks were blowing, and our
neighbors were out watering down their roofs. Our house-
keeper lived in a room at the far end of our house, and because of the danger of fire, my father knocked on her door before he left to help the neighbors. The poor woman thought
he wanted breakfast, and by the time he returned, she had it
on the table. She thought it was a little earlier than usual, but
decided it was not hers to question—just to cook.

"He always began telephoning very early, and there were
many people who wished he would stay in bed longer. Because he was accustomed to having to talk very loudly on the
outmoded ranch telephones, he would also shout on our San
Francisco telephone. I once suggested, 'Why use the telephone? I am sure that if you go outside and yell that loudly,
anyone in this city will hear you.'

"It was interesting to listen to him make a long-distance
telephone call. He would ring the Lovelock operator and
just say, 'Get me Smith in Salt Lake.' Somehow or other she
did it; I guess she had a good memory. He certainly was never
very specific.

"He paid no attention to holidays. If he had business on
his mind, he was quite apt to arrive in Ogden or somewhere
on a Sunday and wonder why no one was in an office. He complained a lot about that.

"He had an office staff, which included a bookkeeper who
took care of most of the financial details. The bookkeeper
would always try to get to the post office each morning before
my father picked up the mail, and there was a good reason for
his efforts. My father often lost things, and he never carried
a notebook. He would write a memorandum on a piece of
paper and stick it in his pocket. One day he was in the Lovelock bank talking to its president, Mr. Pearson, when he pulled

LOVELOCK, NEVADA, IN 1920

a piece of paper from his pocket and started writing a note on it. Mr. Pearson grabbed it from his hand. It was the check for the wool sale—for several hundred thousand dollars.

"When in San Francisco, my father did not spare expense, but aside from that and his clothes, he spent very little money on himself. But he was lavish with his family and very generous with his friends. He always gave big gifts, even in those later years when he really couldn't afford them. He liked silver; he bought cupboards of silver and a great deal of jewelry for my mother. He liked expensive furniture and wanted everything nicely done. He insisted on meals being served promptly, and in our San Francisco house expected gracious service. He enjoyed entertaining fairly small dinner parties at home or at the best restaurants, and he could be quite the polished gentleman when he wanted to be. He liked Scotch whiskey but was never a heavy drinker. He always provided ample liquor to his friends and guests.

"If he didn't like someone, he simply ignored them—just wouldn't discuss them. He often helped people and organizations, but he would not allow his name to be used. A group of Catholic nuns in Winnemucca always received financial help when they needed it, but he tried to keep them from learning where the money came from. He thought they were fine women who did much good work.

"He seemed to be able to get along and communicate with all of the races of people who worked for him—Portugese, Basques, Indians—even though he didn't speak their language. He loved dogs and they seemed to love him. When he walked down a street in Lovelock, it looked like all of the dogs in town were following him. He expected his sheep dogs to be good workers.

"When he drove you in a car, you wished you were walking. He was a terrible driver and he knew absolutely nothing about automobile mechanics. He was always running out of gasoline, and someone at the ranch had to constantly check the gas tank and keep his car in running order.

"One time he bought a new pickup, and as he was driving it near town it stopped running. He walked to a garage where a mechanic, in order to select the proper tools, questioned him in regard to the possible causes of the engine's failure. My father didn't have the slightest idea. When they reached the car the mechanic saw that its motor, because several bolts had not been tightened, had dropped out and was lying on the ground. My father hadn't even noticed.

"My father had a strong temper, but he was never cross with me. I was nineteen, a student at the University of Nevada, when he died."

During his lifetime, John G. Taylor was married twice. His first marriage to Alice Borland in the 1890's brought him two sons, John and Hugh; but ended in divorce when the boys were eight and six years of age. Almost twenty years later he was married again to Helen Gallagher, and in 1921 his daughter, Jeanette, was born. Carmen Taylor Mayes, the daughter of John G's son, Hugh, was adopted by her grandfather and

JEANETTE AND HER HORSE AT LOVELOCK RANCH

lived with him during much of her early life. She thought of him as her father and called him "Dad." Probably she understood him as well as anyone.

"He was absolutely fantastic." Carmen smiled. "We were pals and got along beautifully together. Of course I knew his temperament. He was very quick to get angry; but if you would remain calm and not pay any attention to it, in about ten minutes it was all over and forgotten."

Carmen attended California schools, but her vacations were spent with her grandfather—traveling with him to his many ranches, sheep camps, stock shows and wherever else his business took him. She knew when to talk and when to stay silent; and in many ways she was of help to him.

"Dad was especially particular about the operation of his

ranch kitchens—they had to be clean and food could not be wasted. He always looked in the garbage cans to see what had been thrown away, and I tried to warn every new cook to cover discarded food with paper. Good cooks were hard to find, and if they kept a dirty kitchen or wasted food, they didn't stay long.

"Dad and I would ride into a ranch, and Dad would head for the kitchen. A few minutes later he would take me aside and say, 'The kitchen's dirty, and that damned cook is throwing away good food.'

"I would answer, 'Well, you were the one who hired him and you can fire him.'

"Dad would look a little embarrassed, 'Yeh, but I don't feel in the mood today to fire him. Now, Carmen, you do it.'

"I'd say, 'Darn you, anyway.'

"So then, I'd have to go in and tell the cook, 'Well, you're going on a vacation, I guess. Get your things together, and the foreman will take you into town.'

"And then who would have to get up at 4:00 A.M. to do the cooking for twenty men until a new cook could be found? Yes, it was I—so I'd get in and do it.

"And then in about a week a new cook would arrive, and Dad would say, 'Now, Carmen, you can relax.'

"But I never knew for how long. Cooks came and went pretty fast in the John G. Taylor outfit."

When Carmen was in school, John G. would periodically travel to San Francisco to be with her. "We had lots of fun together," Carmen remembers. "He usually stayed at the Palace or St. Francis hotel, and all of the personnel there knew him and gave him excellent service. Once, when we were at the St. Francis, he told me that when he first came to San Francisco there was a church where the hotel now stands. He said that it was the first place he stopped—to give thanks for having reached the West Coast.

"I would talk Dad into going to the theater. It was easy to get him to go, but it was surely hard to get him to stay. In the middle of the play Dad would rise from his seat and start

"JOHN G." PREPARING A CAMP LUNCH FOR *(left)* MARY MCCULLOCH, NOW MRS.
DUANE MACK, AND CARMEN.

to walk out while saying in a loud voice, 'Very good, very good.'

"I would make him sit down, reminding him that he had promised to stay through the whole play. And he would whisper, 'I'll stay, I'll stay.'

"Pretty soon he would start to squirm, and I would feel those long legs going back and forth and cross and recross; and he would say, 'How long is this thing going to last?'

"Finally I would feel sorry for him and we would leave.

"However, one time we went to see Harry Lauder at the Curran. He didn't have any trouble staying that time. At the end he asked, 'Well, isn't there going to be some more? How about staying to see it over again?'

"Dad could speak Gaelic; he had learned it when he was young. He had two friends who also spoke it, and they would get together once a year and drink their Scotch and Soda and speak nothing else.

"They would laugh; you've never heard such laughter, and with Gaelic, you've never heard such a conglomeration. They just laughed it up and would have a ball. Dad just loved it.

"Dad was always very generous with his family and everyone, but I've never known him to be at a Christmas tree. I think it embarrassed him; he had never had it when he was young. And I have never seen him open a gift. When he was given a package he would say, 'Oh, that's lovely,' but he would never open it. It was always stored in one of his closets on a shelf. But sometimes when we were alone, if he thought that he needed some socks or a tie or something, he would take me to the closet and point to a package and say, 'Carmen, how about looking in that one. It looks like a tie box or a socks box. Why don't you open a few of them?'

"I never really understood why he wouldn't open his presents himself.

"Oddly enough, Dad never learned any Basque swear words although many Basque people worked for him. But I did learn them, and sometimes they came in handy—like the time he went off for two weeks and left me to cook for his guests and ranch hands, twenty-four people altogether. When he returned I used some good Basque swear words. It was fortunate that he did not understand them.

"Dad was very lenient with me, but when he corrected me I knew he meant business; and I didn't contradict him. I do remember one time that he accused me of something, and he was wrong. I showed my temper that time, and he smiled and said, 'By God, you're a Taylor.'

"He said he was sorry; it was the only time I ever heard him apologize.

"Dad was an awful driver. He had a lot of accidents, and he tried to keep us from knowing about them. When he got into trouble he'd always say, 'Don't tell anybody.'

"One day he was sailing along in a Dodge car on the way to the I L ranch. The road was narrow with a steep embankment on one side. His men were putting up the ranch's hay and his mind was on that. He was looking out over the fields; he didn't see the sharp turn in the road ahead. Well, he just kept going straight, went over the embankment; and the car rolled over twice before landing upright.

"One of the ranch hands came running up, calling, 'Are you all right, Mr. Taylor?'

"Dad got out of the car; he didn't have a scratch, 'Why, yes —I'm fine. That was quite an experience, I kind of enjoyed it. But don't tell anybody. I'll fire you if you do.'

"Another day, on one of Lovelock's main streets, he was driving on the inside lane when he suddenly decided to turn to the right. He hit a gasoline truck and turned it over on its side. He jumped out and told the driver, 'I'll pay all the damages—anything. But don't let this get around. Don't tell anybody.'

"He was not only a terrible driver, but he probably had more flat tires than anyone in Pershing, Humboldt, or Elko county. So he decided to stop that; and, against everyone's advice, he took his Buick touring car into a Winnemucca garage and had it equipped with solid, hard-rubber tires, the kind which had holes through the sides. I told him he would be sorry, but he wouldn't listen.

"Well, it was shearing time, and he had to drive up a grade

on a narrow dirt road to the shearing corrals at Shafer Springs. I was following him in another car, and as he climbed the hill his car with the hard, rubber tires began skidding back and forth, almost going over the edge. He was scared, but he wouldn't stop—wouldn't admit that he had been wrong.

"But when he got back to Winnemucca, he made a beeline for the garage. He told the owner, 'By God, I almost killed myself going up to that damned Shafer Springs. Put my old tires back on—but don't tell anybody.' "

It was John G. Taylor's temper which provided the theme for most of the old stories.

Carmen recalls, "When he lost his temper he would take his hat off and throw it on the ground and stomp on it. He could be in a bank; he could be anywhere—he would take that hat and throw it down and stomp on it and swear a blue streak. It wasn't the big things he'd lose his temper over—usually he wouldn't bat an eyelash about them. It was the little things which would set him off.

"One day when I was with him, he accepted the delivery of a new automobile from a dealer in Winnemucca. The salesman told him how to operate the car, and Dad and I drove out into the desert to see some land in which he was interested. If he wanted to go to some place where there wasn't a road he would take off through the sagebrush.

"Well, we were about three miles from a ranch when the car stalled. He tried to start the engine, but it wouldn't run. He kept trying, and he began getting angrier and angrier. Finally he lost his temper.

"He grabbed the gear shift and started pushing it in all directions. And then he pulled straight up on it, and the lever came out of its socket. He opened the car door and threw the lever as far as he could throw it. Then he turned to me, 'What did you say the name of this damned car is?'

"I told him the name.

"He said, 'I'll never drive one of these things again, and if I ever find one on any of my ranches, I'll skin the son of a b - - - - who bought it.

"He left me there and walked to the ranch. Walking was the best way for him to cool his temper—he could always walk it off.

"He was really something."

Paul Flanigan, son of the Nevada sheepman, Pat Flanigan, served as Taylor's superintendent from 1926 through 1929, and he also remembers his employer's temper.

"Mr. Taylor and I went to dinner at the Humboldt Hotel where he made his headquarters when he was in Winnemucca. As a specialty, the restaurant was serving buffalo steak. I asked Mr. Taylor if he wanted to tackle it, and he said, 'I've never eaten any, let's try it.'

"The waitress brought it in; it was tougher than dried cowhide. Mr. Taylor blew up, yelled at the waitress, and went up to his room.

"A few minutes later he came back down, walked by me without a word, and went into the restaurant where he apologized to the waitress.

"For him to apologize was unheard of, but he made up for it on the way back. As he crossed the lobby he happened to notice the hotel manager talking to several guests. He turned and walked over to him and, in an even voice, said, 'Bradley, if you ever serve me any of that goddamned buffalo meat again, I'm through with your goddamned hotel.'

"On another day, I was with Mr. Taylor and Mr. E. P. Ellison. Together they had purchased a large ranch holding which had been a part of the Union Land and Cattle Company and which included the great Spanish ranch. They were dividing the land between them, and after two weeks of negotiation, everything seemed to be settled. I was driving them along the boundary between their two properties when we came to an old stove. Mr. Taylor turned to me and said, 'Send a wagon up after that stove.'

"Mr. Ellison was a quiet man, of the Mormon religion, who never swore. He looked over at John G. and mildly protested, 'Now, Mr. Taylor, that stove is on my property.'

"They argued about it for several minutes, and finally Mr. Taylor lost his temper. He threw his hat on the ground, jumped on it, and said, 'I'll be damned if that's your stove.'

"I knew the war was about to begin. After two weeks of hard work dividing the property, an old kitchen stove was about to blow up the whole deal. I'm feeling helpless; I just have to listen and wonder what will happen. I could talk to Mr. Ellison; but, until he calmed down, I couldn't talk to Mr. Taylor—and I'm working for Mr. Taylor.

"Mr. Ellison walked outside and I started to follow him.

"Mr. Taylor called, 'Where are you going?'

" 'I'm going outside; I've had about enough of this. Here you're dividing up a million-dollar property, and you're in a big fight over a lousy kitchen stove.'

"So I went out and talked to Mr. Ellison. I said, 'There's a lot of money at stake. Mr. Taylor won't change his mind— can you let him have the stove?'

"He thought for a minute and with a shrug agreed, 'I guess you're right; let him have it.'

"So I went back in to tell Mr. Taylor, but before I could say a word he bellowed, 'Go tell that damned preacher to take that damned stove.'

"Then he went for a walk."

There is little doubt that the temper of John G. Taylor was widely known. Mrs. Avery Stitser, former owner and editor of Winnemucca's *Humboldt Star* newspaper, remembers the day that she happened to meet him at the Winnemucca railroad depot. "He had been up to some of his northern ranches and was waiting to board a train to return to Lovelock.

"He was a very prominent man throughout the West; and, like everyone else, I had great respect and admiration for him.

"I had met him once when I was a small girl. I remember that he shook hands with me; and as he released my hand I said, 'Oh! Look at the dirt on my hand. I apologize.'

"Then he again took my hand in his and gently said, 'That's a hand of work. That's the kind I like.'

"Well, this day, years later, when I met him at the depot, the newspapers were filled with the Prince of Wales-Wally Simpson story. Our conversation happened to touch on that, and I said that I agreed with the British government that the Prince of Wales must step down. I soon realized that Mr. Taylor entirely disagreed. But I stuck to my guns and we argued rather heatedly.

"And then something I had often heard about and always wanted to see occurred. Mr. Taylor took off his hat, threw it on the ground, and jumped on it.

"I was delighted."

John G. Taylor was one of the few large ranchers who successfully ran cattle and sheep in the same operation. He had no patience with arguments between his sheepherders and his buckaroos, believing that, if managed correctly, there should be no conflict between the two kinds of livestock ranching. Where the sheep were concerned, John G. made all of the decisions, but generally he did not interfere with his cattle boss.

Paul Flanigan, however, remembers an exception to that policy.

"We were at the Clover ranch where Mr. Taylor had decided to sell the older cows along with their calves. The buckaroos were working the cattle with horses, separating the older ones from the others. This takes time and patience because the calves must stay with their own mothers.

"Well, Mr. Taylor thought it was going too slowly, and he came boiling through the gate of the corral carrying two long willow sticks. He yelled at the cowhands, 'Get those horses out of this goddamned corral.'

"He turned to me and, handing me one of the willows, ordered, 'You stand in the gate. When I get the cow and the calf I want, get out of the way.'

"It wasn't very long before he had most of the calves mismothered and everything else in a state of confusion. I said to him, 'Hold it a minute. You're cutting out the wrong calf

with each cow. You want to sell those calves and cows correctly paired—is that right.'

"He answered, 'That's right.'

"I said, 'Then let somebody get in there who knows what
he's doing.'

"John G. looked at me like he was about ready to start
throwing his fists. 'Who owns these goddamned cows, you or
me?'

"I said, 'You do.'

"Well, then, I'm going to do just as I goddamned please.'

"The next day, when Mr. Taylor had moved on to another
ranch, the riders and I did it all over again and got the calves
back to their mothers.

"Among his employees and others, John G. had a reputation
of being very tough; and, in some respects, he was. He would
fire a man at the drop of a hat, but usually he would hire him
back the next day. He was a man you had to know well to
understand. He was temperamental and highly strung, but
I have seen him do this. I had his checkbook when I worked
for him; and he would be sitting in the Humboldt Hotel; and
he would see an old-timer, a former employee, across the lobby; and he would say to me, 'Go give that fellow fifty dollars.'

"He didn't want the man to know he had given the money.
He did many things like that.

"But when he lost his temper, he would tackle anyone.
When he would drive into one of his ranches, I could tell if
he spotted something wrong, and Lord help the man who was
responsible. One day on a ranch near Golconda a Portugese
employee was burning green cottonwood in the kitchen stove.
When Mr. Taylor went in the house it was full of smoke and
Mr. Taylor lost his temper. One thing led to another, and
the employee hit John G. over the head with a piece of the
green cottonwood. The blow raised a lump on his head that
remained there as long as I knew him.

"He couldn't stand garlic, and most of his sheepherders
and cowhands used garlic. If any cook on his ranches served
garlic on his food, he was liable to tear the place apart.

"But when he lost his temper, if you left him alone he

would go for a walk and in a short time he would be all right again.

"John G. was a great walker. If he and I were out someplace and the truck would get stuck or break down, he would start walking, and it didn't make any difference how far it was to his next ranch. If I did get the truck started and caught up with him, I would see him walking down the road, sometimes stopping here and there to throw a rock to the side—clearing the road.

"Often when he was walking across the desert from one sheep camp to another, he would cut over to the railroad tracks. A limited train would come along and he would flag it down. The train would come to a halt and the engineer would lean out of the cab and say, 'Hello, Mr. Taylor—get on.'

"The conductor would be waiting for him on the steps of a passenger car, and John G. would pat his hip pocket and say, 'By God, I don't have my wallet. Get the fare from my bookkeeper in Lovelock.'

"And the conductor would say, 'All right, Mr. Taylor. Make yourself comfortable—where would you like to get off?'[2]

"It may seem impossible that a limited train would stop out on the desert like that, but all of the train crews knew John G. Taylor—it seemed like everyone knew him."

Taylor trailed his sheep each year from his winter range in the Lovelock Valley to the summer range in northeastern Nevada. Bands of about two thousand head each moved slowly along established trails and were followed, during the earlier years, by big freight wagons pulled by mule or horse teams.

Mr. Reginald Meaker, of Reno, who, as a representative of the Draper Company of Boston, bought Taylor wool, states that John G. was "one of the most knowledgeable men in the sheep business in the western United States. His sheep were of the Merino breed with strictly fine wool, and Taylor's close personal supervision assured their thorough care.

---

2. John G. Taylor's ability to flag down limited trains in the middle of the desert was mentioned in a Reno newspaper article written at the time of his death. It was also recently verified by a retired Southern Pacific Railroad engineer.

"His concern for his sheep, however, also resulted in diffi-
culties during the shearing season. Sheepshearers were spe-
cialists in the sheep business, recruited by a 'captain' who con-
tracted with ranchers for their services. In those days they
used hand shears to remove the wool, and because the Merino's
skin was so heavily wrinkled it was almost impossible to shear
a band without nicking at least one. Actually, a cut healed
so quickly that it couldn't be seen in ten days. But every time
John G. saw blood on a sheep, he fired the shearing crew. It
was said that he never averaged less than three crews each
season."

In the early days most of the Taylor employees were Portugese. Later he also hired Basques and Indians. Charlie
Thompson, an Indian, was with him almost fifty years and at
one time had charge of part of his cattle operation. Most of
Taylor's permanent employees respected his strength and
understood his temper. They were loyal to him and he was
loyal to them. The authors of *Nevada's Northeast Frontier*[3]
wrote, "At one time a Basque herder seeking U.S. citizenship
upon being asked who was President of the United States answered, 'John G. Taylor.' "

In 1911 Taylor brought the orphaned children of his broth-
er, a boy and two girls, from Scotland to the United States.
He provided a house for them in San Francisco and had them
attend school there. The boy, Hugh, had the same first name
as John G.'s younger son.

Hugh Taylor, who currently lives in the Lovelock Valley,
remembers his uncle as, "very bright and very quick in movement. He never talked about himself; he had little time to
talk; he was always busy with his work. He was afraid of no
one—he would tell you to go to hell as fast as he would look
at you. He kept his business to himself. He once told me,
'If somebody asks you a personal question, instead of answer-
ing, ask him one.'

"He was a very fine man, very kind and generous to me and
my sisters. I worked for him for more than four years. My

---

3. Patterson, Ulph, and Goodwin, *Nevada's Northeast Frontier* (Sparks, Nev.: Western Printing and Publishing Co., 1969) .

JOHN G. TAYLOR'S SHEEP WERE NOTED FOR THEIR FINE WOOL

job included hiring some of the men, taking care of the pay-
roll, paying the bills, and buying the food and other supplies
for the ranches.

"All of the food was bought in carload lots. Once a year,
in the last of December, he would tell me, 'I want all of the
ranches stocked with good substantial food. Get bids from
several grocers for the whole supply; I don't want to see you
in any store buying small amounts. I want you to talk to my
blacksmiths and order what they need in round and flat iron
and wagon wheel spokes and all of that. And get what salt
we will need for the sheep during the year. Buy everything
on bids.'

"That's the way he operated his ranches—efficiently, fru-
gally.

"When I first went to work I wore a cap, and I wanted to
get a hat—the kind they wore here in Nevada. I told my uncle, and he went to the Golden Rule store and bought me a

big western hat for about a dollar and a half. When I put it on, the men on the ranch laughed at me and I heard John G. Taylor say, 'My nephew looks like a bandit in that hat.'

"I got a little angry at all that. My uncle took me aside and said to me, 'When I first herded sheep I wore a piece of barley sack for a hat; I didn't have a dollar and a half to buy one.' Then he threw his good beaver hat on the ground and stepped on it.

"I understood what he was telling me—that you had to work for what you get and that I had to learn values. It wasn't that he was not generous. He was very good to me—he would give me almost anything.

"On another occasion he gave his son, Jack, and me each a pair of shoes and some socks. The shoes were heavy and stiff and too large. Jack threw his out the door and I sold mine to another employee.

"My uncle learned what I had done with the shoes and he said to me, 'I tried to do you a favor.'

"I answered, 'They were too large.'

"He said, 'Why didn't you put on an extra pair of socks?'

"He never bought me another pair of shoes.

"One day I had to go into Lovelock to pick up a new employee. I hitched a black horse and a black colt, which was partly broke, up to the buckboard. When I arrived in town and stopped in front of the saloon where the new man was supposed to meet me, I saw John G. Taylor across the street. He was waiting for a train, and I noticed that he was watching me. Just at that moment the train pulled into town and blew its whistle. The noise frightened the colt and it jumped over the tongue of the wagon, landing alongside the other horse. I was holding the reins wondering what to do when the train's whistle blew again and the colt jumped back over the tongue to where it belonged.

"My uncle walked across the street and said, 'That was fine horsemanship, Hugh.' And he handed me a twenty-dollar gold piece.

"He had a sense of humor. One time Jack and I drank some Scotch whiskey which was in a small keg that he kept in his office. We thought we should substitute something in place of the whiskey to make the barrel heavier so we poured in some vinegar. After my uncle returned home, he had a drink one evening. We expected the worst; but apparently he found it humorous. However, the next time he left town he told the foreman to be sure that the boys had plenty of work to keep them busy.

"Sometimes he would give me fifty dollars and say, 'You are doing fine, Hugh.' Then he would add, 'You can use this to buy a new hat.'

"He never forgot the hat that made me look like a bandit.

"My uncle didn't like me to smoke. He told me, 'If the Lord wanted you to smoke he would have built a chimney in your head.'

"One time I said to my uncle, 'I would like to have a piece of property that I can call my own.'

"I pointed out a small area of land and told him that I would like to buy it.

"He turned his back to me and was silent for a few minutes. Then he said, 'I can't sell or give you any of my property, Hugh. I want to own all of the land that I can obtain.'

"He gave me everything that I wanted; he spent more than ten thousand dollars on me; but he couldn't give up his land.

"Once he said to me, 'Someday I'm going to Scotland where I was born, and I'm going to take you with me to show me around.'

"He never went."

John G. Taylor's life was not free of tragedy. He had hoped that his younger son, Hugh (Carmen's father), would carry on his ranching empire. Carmen remembers, "Both of his sons were very bright. They were offered appointments to West Point, but they wouldn't go. Hugh was a calm type who got along with his father.

"Hugh loved horses, raced cars, flew airplanes—did everything. During World War I he enlisted in the cavalry, but because of his flying experience he was transferred to the Air

Force. He had many friends; and their parties would start in Lovelock or Fallon, continue in Reno, go on to San Francisco, and end up at Del Monte.

"In 1923 he died following surgery. He was twenty-eight years old."

It was nine years later, in 1932, that John G. Taylor lost his great ranches. Probably his unquenchable desire to expand his holdings kept him from retrenching before the depression brought a critical decline in livestock prices and a consequent inability to meet operating and loan expenses. He fought to keep his land, but he lost.

Jeanette recalls, "As difficult as it must have been, it was not something that he talked much about. And there was never any self-pity or criticism."

Mrs. Avery Stitser remembers, "A man who realized the extent of Mr. Taylor's losses asked him how he felt about giving up his properties. Mr. Taylor answered, 'My ranches may be gone, but no one will ever take away the pleasure I had in building them.'"

John G. Taylor's career was not ended. Property in the name of his daughter-in-law, Wanda Taylor (Carmen's mother), was not affected by the foreclosures, and at the age of seventy-eight Taylor began rebuilding. The *Humboldt Star* newspaper reported,

"Taylor was not to be downed by the loss of his millions, the crumbling of a fortune it took him more than two score of years to build. He started all over again and developed the Wanda Taylor interests, and in Humboldt county again at the Hot Springs ranch was building a huge area of ranch land."

In the late thirties Roy Hardy visited him at the Hot Springs ranch. "He took George Wingfield and me around his property and pointed out what he intended to do in the future. He was then eighty-four or eighty-five years old. To accomplish his plans would have taken twenty years—and he expected to do it."

In 1940, Gladys Rowley wrote in her *Nevada State Journal* newspaper column, "Reno Revue,"

"It is not my good fortune to know John G. Taylor, but I have heard older Nevadans speak of him often. In years not so long past, his name was always there when the roll of the state's most distinguished men was called.

"It is still there.

"For years he was known as the biggest landowner in the state. His far-reaching acres were an empire, as big as many states. His cattle and sheep were almost countless.

"Then came a series of evil happenings. One dry year after another. Stock dying on the ranges and in what once was green pastures. No market for what was left. Panic. Obligations which had to be met. What had been an imperial domain was broken, and John G. Taylor was not a young man anymore.

"Not young in years—but very sturdy in brain and body. He set about repairing the varied ravages of uncontrollable forces. He rode the far ranges as of old. At break of dawn he'd appear unexpectedly, in some lonely camp. He was looking things over.

"He still does that—and he is 86 years old. He wears out the younger men in his employ as, tirelessly, he goes from place to place—looking over the land, seeing to it that the stock are provided for. Thousands of acres belong to him again. His ambition: to rebuild the vast kingdom that once was his.

"In the old days his name was always being mentioned in connection with a Governorship or a United States Senatorship. He was deaf to all those alluring offers. His place, he would say, was on the range.

"Of late he has been working so quietly—though intensely —that even some of his close friends have missed seeing his name in the papers now and then. They haven't even heard about him. And they have wondered.

"They need have no anxiety. John G. Taylor is 86 years

old—but he has the stamina of youth. He is ceaselessly planning. And some of his plans, I am told, will take 15 years for consummation.

"He is one of Nevada's Big men. And those who know him well, and those who know him only by repute, salute him, wish him well."

Such was John G. Taylor—tough, gentle, frugal, generous, temperamental, individualistic—who built a ranching empire in the Nevada desert.

As Carmen phrased it, "He was really something."

CHAPTER VII

Sanctuary

FOR THOSE PEOPLE who visit the Nevada desert but wish to travel only on improved roads, most of the desert's spectacular beauty and places of interest are available. Principal highways bisect the length and width of the state, and paved or graded gravel roads branch from them to all general regions.

Western history buffs will find that the country through which long stretches of the old emigrant trails passed can be seen while driving main highways. Our modern engineers apparently agreed with the routes selected by the early scouts, for Interstate Highway 80 parallels the California Trail across most of the state, and U.S. Highway 91 follows much of the Old Spanish Trail from the Utah line to Las Vegas.

Markers point out historical sites, and museums in some of the larger and smaller cities of the state preserve artifacts of the desert's past. An official highway map, which can be obtained from the Nevada State Highway Department in Carson City, provides information about public campgrounds and places of interest throughout Nevada.*

The Nevada State Park System has preserved several of the desert's areas of unusual beauty and some of its historical and recreational sites. Photographs and brief descriptions of these interesting areas follow.

In addition to the people who enjoy the desert while driving improved roads, there are those who travel to the more remote areas. With four-wheel drive or other suitable vehicles, they follow the old emigrant trails, collect rocks, hunt game, or just enjoy the beauty and solitude of the primitive country. To

---

*An excellent pamphlet, "Your Guide to Camping in Nevada," may be obtained free of charge by writing the Nevada State Park System, Carson, City, Nevada 89701.

Courtesy Nevada State Highway Department

THE VALLEY OF FIRE STATE PARK IN CLARK COUNTY, WITH ITS BEAUTIFUL RED SAND-
STONE CARVED INTO BIZARRE FORMS BY EROSION AND ITS PETROGLYPHS, IS ONE OF THE
MOST UNUSUAL SCENIC AREAS IN THE SOUTHERN DESERT. THE LOST CITY MUSEUM IS
LOCATED IN OVERTON, A SHORT DISTANCE FROM THE PARK.

Courtesy Nevada State Highway Department

CATHEDRAL GORGE STATE PARK IN LINCOLN COUNTY IS A BEAUTIFUL AND UNUSUAL
NARROW VALLEY ENCLOSED BY HIGH, PERPENDICULAR WALLS OF BENTONITE CLAY FOR-
MATIONS. EROSION THROUGH COUNTLESS CENTURIES HAS FORMED DIVERSIFIED DESIGNS
INCLUDING MAGNIFICENT SPIRES RESEMBLING THOSE OF A CATHEDRAL.

THE BERLIN-ICHTHYOSAUR STATE PARK, TWENTY-THREE MILES EAST OF GABBS, CONTAINS THE PETRIFIED BONES OF GIANT WATER REPTILES WHICH LIVED IN A SEA WHICH EXTENDED OVER WESTERN NEVADA MORE THAN SEVENTY MILLION YEARS AGO.

THE WARD CHARCOAL OVENS HISTORIC STATE MONUMENT, FIFTEEN MILES SOUTH OF ELY, ALLOWS VISITORS TO EXAMINE THE EXCELLENT CONSTRUCTION OF THE BEEHIVE-SHAPED OVENS USED BY EARLY-DAY SMELTERS TO MAKE CHARCOAL.

OLDEST LOG CABIN IN NEVADA AT GENOA NEV.

THE MORMON STATION HISTORIC STATE MONUMENT AT GENOA IS ON THE SITE OF
NEVADA'S OLDEST SETTLEMENT.

THE KERSHAW-RYAN STATE PARK, THREE MILES SOUTH OF CALIENTE, OFFERS PICK-
NICKERS AND CAMPERS A PLEASANT OAK FOREST SURROUNDED BY GRAPEVINE-COVERED
CLIFFS.

Courtesy Nevada State Park System
THE EAGLE VALLEY STATE RECREATION AREA PROVIDES BOATING AND FISHING FOR ITS VISITORS, AS WELL AS CAMPING AND PICKNICKING FACILITIES. IT IS LOCATED TWENTY-TWO MILES EAST OF PIOCHE.

Courtesy Nevada Fish and Game Commission
THE BEAVER DAM STATE PARK IN LINCOLN COUNTY LIES IN A SETTING OF PINE FORESTS AND LOFTY CLIFFS.

FORT CHURCHILL HISTORIC STATE MONUMENT, TWENTY-FIVE MILES FROM YERINGTON, PRESERVES THE RUINS OF AN ARMY OUTPOST ESTABLISHED IN 1860 FOLLOWING THE TWO BATTLES OF PYRAMID LAKE.*

those who understand the desert it is a pleasant type of recreation, but to the inadequately equipped beginner it can be a rugged and even dangerous experience. On trips into isolated areas, the condition of the vehicle is especially important. In the heat and dust of the desert, mechanical failures are not uncommon; and good tires, extra engine oil, a spare fan belt, an extra set of radiator hoses, tools, a large heavy-duty jack, and a separate container of water for emergency use in the car's radiator are probably minimum necessities. A few planks carried along may be worth the space they take when crossing playas where there may be mud or sand.

Traveling in a party of two or more cars is one of the best safety factors; but, when that is not possible, some Nevadans

---

*Three additional State Recreational Areas of the Nevada Park System are located at Lahontan Reservoir, south of Fernley, Rye Patch Reservoir, east of Lovelock, and Echo Canyon Reservoir, east of Pioche.

ORGANIZED BY CEDARVILLE, CALIFORNIA, PEOPLE, A GROUP OF EMIGRANT TRAIL BUFFS FROM NEVADA, NORTHEASTERN CALIFORNIA, AND SOUTHERN OREGON FOLLOWED THE LASSEN-APPLEGATE TRAIL DURING THE PAST TWO SUMMERS.

IN CASE OF ENGINE FAILURE, A TRAIL BIKE OF SOME TYPE CARRIED IN THE BACK OF THE CAR ADDS A SAFETY FACTOR ON TRIPS INTO REMOTE AREAS OF THE DESERT.

carry a small, motorized trail bike in the rear of their pickup or station wagon. And realizing that regardless of all precautions, the unexpected may still occur, it is wise to leave word with someone at home of the general area of the trip in case a search becomes necessary.

In the earlier days of Nevada, when travel was limited to horse or foot, stories of becoming lost in the desert were common; but few realize how often it happens today. The desert offers signposts for the return journey—an odd-shaped peak on the skyline, a green patch on a mountainside, and other natural nonconformities unusual enough to be remembered and prominent enough to be kept in sight. But more than one experienced hunter or hiker has neglected to note landmarks and spent uncomfortable hours trying to find his camp or car.

There is more than one reason for carrying a set of topographic maps[1] in the automobile when traveling unfamiliar areas, but the following illustrates a good one. In an isolated section of northern Nevada several summers ago a station wagon broke through a playa's surface crust to sink into deep mud. After several hours of unsuccessfully attempting to extract the vehicle, the driver decided to abandon it and follow the car's tracks back to a settlement he had passed earlier that morning. Ten hot hours and thirty long miles later, he reached his destination—to learn that a mining community lay just over the hill from where he had left his car.

It is obvious that an ample supply of drinking water should be carried on an expedition into arid country; but emergencies sometimes occur, and desert travelers have been interested in a method of obtaining survival water[2] which requires only a plastic sheet[3] and a watertight container, such as a quart can.

Where it will receive the heat of the sun's rays, a hole about forty inches in diameter is dug to a depth of about two feet.

---

1. United States Geological Survey and Army Map Service topographic maps are excellent for back-road and cross-country travel.
2. For more detailed directions on this method of obtaining water, see Douglas, Ernest, "Water for Survival Is Everywhere If You Can Get It," *Desert Magazine*, October, 1965.
3. The plastic should be of a type to which droplets of water will adhere.

Old Conveyor Belts Are Used To Cross the Bottomless Mud of a Spring Runoff Stream on the Black Rock Desert.

In Case the Conveyor Belt Experiment Is a Failure, There Will Still Be Two Cars on Solid Ground To Pull the First One Out of the Mud.

The container is lowered to the center of the bottom of the hole, and the plastic sheet is then stretched over the excavation and anchored along its sides with rocks and dirt. A stone large enough to cause the plastic to sag from its weight is then placed on the sheet directly above the container.

Air trapped in the hole gathers moisture from the soil around it, and this moisture condenses on the underside of the plastic sheet, trickles to its lowest point, and drips into the container. The amount of water this "desert still" will produce varies with certain conditions, but usually is enough for survival.

One or more of the canyons surrounding a Great Basin Desert valley often contain a spring or small stream. These areas where water is either on or near the surface can usually be located from a distance by the brighter green color of the plant life around them.

Certain regions of the Nevada desert can be hazardous. The human body can withstand only a limited amount of dehydration, and during the summer months large areas of the Mohave Desert have temperatures in excess of 120° Fahrenheit. Man has the ability to devise ways of surviving in unfavorable environments for long periods of time; and panic, which eliminates sensible thinking, is probably the cause of many deaths in arid country.

To those who understand and respect the desert, it is a friendly, beautiful part of this earth; and there is an interesting challenge in learning to live comfortably in its environment. A desert camp can have many of the luxuries of home when ice boxes, gasoline stoves, down sleeping bags, specially constructed water containers, and even comfortable folding chairs go along on the trip. Canvas tarps or one of the new aluminized plastic sheets originally developed for aerospace insulation are helpful in providing shade or windbreaks.

When darkness comes to the desert, the temperature drops quickly. On barren playas, where fuel for a campfire is scarce, a few logs brought along in the back of the car can add to the camp's comfort and pleasantness.

And finally, mention must be made of that all-important

Equipment To Make a Comfortable Camp Adds to the Enjoyment of a Desert Trip.

Courtesy Dave Basso
The High Desert's Hillsides Shine with the Silvery Gray of Its Sagebrush

guy, the experienced camp cook, whose charcoal-broiled steaks surpass the cooking of the world's great chefs.

It has been said that the tenderfoot roughs it, and the experienced outdoorsman lives in comfort.

Probably no one knows the extent of mankind's need for periodic contact with a natural environment. Undoubtedly the desire varies greatly in individuals, but it seems certain that to many Americans the term recreation includes the opportunity of visiting the outdoors.

Most of the Nevada desert is public land. Managed for "multiple use," it has served ranching and mining interests yet remained publicly owned and of benefit to many people. During recent years economic and other forces for transferring federal lands to private ownership have increased.

Throughout the West there is fear of the unscrupulous promoter-speculator who develops land without concern for its wisest use. His past record has proved the necessity of careful planning, with consideration for those long-range needs of all interests, before public ownership of large areas are relinquished.

To those who love the desert, its beauty and primitive qualities are unique and precious. To them it is a world of stillness, of vast space, of great mountains with canyons so sharp and deep that the sun's rays hardly touch their floors. It is a region of brightness where rocks and plants, scrubbed by windblown sand, sparkle with their cleanliness. It is a land of mystery where ancient man left evidence of his visits thousands of years ago. It is a place of history where Indian warriors fought for their way of life, and where legends of the old West were born.

Because of man's alterations, the Nevada desert is no longer a true natural area; but it is still a refuge for some special living things—wild animals and plants which are unable to survive in a tamed environment. And to some men, those who love wilderness and need solitude, it is also a sanctuary.

"And he came to the desert, and there he found peace."

Appendix A

THIS INFORMATION concerning rattlesnake venom was prepared by William A. O'Brien III, M.D., after discussions and other personal communications with Dr. Findlay E. Russell, Director of Laboratory and Professor of Neurological Research, University of Southern California School of Medicine.

"It was not uncommon for certain Indian tribes to have rattlesnakes bite into the livers of other animals, particularly deer, for the purpose of extracting venom. After the animal had been killed and the liver obtained, several snakes would be induced to bite into it, hopefully and supposedly injecting venom. That venom was injected under these circumstances is most likely.

"The liver was then buried and a certain amount of putrefaction allowed to take place. Later the decomposed liver was dug up and smeared on arrow points. This foul material contained not only venom but unquestionably a multitudinous host of bacteria. Although the Indians thought the burying process increased the toxicity of the venom, there is no evidence for this, nor has the problem been pursued in experimental circles. In all probability humans injured by arrow points smeared with this material would suffer, at the least, a greater hazard of severe crippling or death-dealing infection than they would toxic reaction to the snake venom.

"Both liver and snake venom contain a variety of enzyme systems. When mixed together one cannot say with certainty what the result of their interactions and reactions would be with regard to the toxicity of the venom.

"Dr. Findlay E. Russell has in his possession rattlesnake venom aged and preserved for over fifty years. Although some of its enzyme systems have broken down during this time, the venom retains its toxicity. In other words, it is basically very stable.

"Dr. Russell further relates the history of a child cut on a fence where rattlesnakes had been "milked" many months previously. The child suffered the toxic reactions of a rattlesnake bite—attesting to the basic stability of the venom even when it had been dried and exposed to the elements.

"It is further known that primitive people in many parts of the world were accustomed to placing the liver of a small animal or fowl on a snake bite in the belief that this was somehow beneficial. How it may have been beneficial is again speculative and needs laboratory study to affirm or deny.

"Thus there were two divergent methods of liver usage employed by people of earlier times for specific purposes when dealing with snake venom:

1. Liver impregnated venom as a means of enhancing (?) toxicity;

2. Liver applied to snake bites as a means of decreasing (?) toxicity. Neither method is in necessary conflict with the other.

"One thing history has taught us repeatedly is that we should not discount the validity of ancient practices without adequate proof to the contrary."

Appendix B

THROUGH the cooperation of Mr. David A. Gibson, Old Military Records Division, National Archives, Washington, D.C., and Mr. Joseph T. McDonnell, a search of 1865-66 Nevada military records produced forty-one handwritten documents consisting mostly of journals and reports from field commanders to superior officers at Fort Churchill. Muster rolls, made available by Frederic C. Gale, Nevada State Archivist, were also studied.

Information from these primary sources not only verify much of the material obtained from the old newspapers but also provide additional understanding of the events and persons involved in this period of conflict in the Nevada desert.

Footnotes in the text refer to the following:

(A) No mention of any consequent investigation of the March 14 engagement at Winnemucca Lake was found in the military records. Though incidental, it was interesting to learn from the muster rolls that in 1865 Captain A. (Almond) B. Wells was only twenty-three years of age.

(B) Lieutenant R. A. Osmer, Second Cavalry, California Volunteers, in his report of his November 17 fight "in the vicinity of the Black Rock Mountains" stated, "These Indians are 'Bannocks,' and the same who killed and robbed the teamster 35 miles from this post. . . ."

However, on December 18, Lieutenant Osmer wrote, "I have this day recd [*sic*] a letter from Thomas Stark, a citizen living on the Humboldt River, at Smiths Crossing, who informs me that Capt Tom and two of his tribe of Indians, the same I had the fight with on the 17th of November 1865, have come to his place and surrendered themselves and sued for peace."

These are two pages from Captain A. B. Wells' journal of the march of his command of sixty men from Camp McDermit, Paradise Valley, to the table mountain where he was defeated by Indian forces on May 20, 1865.

Many references point out that "Capt. Tom" and "Black Rock Tom" were names for the same person and that he was a Paiute Indian.

Primary sources offer convincing evidence that the bands of Indians raiding travelers and settlers and fighting military forces across northern Nevada were made up of Bannocks, Paiutes, and possibly some Shoshones; and that these bands were organized, at least loosely, to form a united force against the whites.

(C) Official military records not always agreed with newspaper accounts. The *Humboldt Register* reported fifty-five known Indian casualties in the Black Rock battle of November 17; but Lieutenant Osmer stated that one hundred and twenty Indians were killed.

(D) Four field reports written by Lieutenant Colonel Charles McDermit, Commanding Officer of the Military District of Nevada, establish that during June and July of 1865 he was making a determined and courageous attempt to bring peace to northern Nevada. The reports (dated June 9, June 15, July 1, and August 2) tell the story of an expedition which, in regard to distances traveled and numbers of men involved, was a remarkable undertaking.

According to his report of June 9, Colonel McDermit, accompanied by Nevada Governor H. G. Blasdel and an escort of cavalry, left Fort Churchill on May 30 en route to Austin. At the latter settlement they met and talked to "100" Indians in an attempt to encourage them to "separate from the hostile, be peaceable and they would be protected."

On June 4, Colonel McDermit traveled northward through mountainous country where ranches and dwellings were deserted because of the Indian threat. Intersecting the Humboldt River seventy miles above Unionville, he had begun to meet and collect into his command other companies of cavalry and mounted infantry already in the field. By June 12, when Captain Wells and his command arrived, the total force had increased to over four hundred* men including Indian scouts.

---

*The *Humboldt Register* newspaper stated that Colonel McDermit had a command of six hundred men. According to McDermit's reports, the five commands

Continuing in a northerly direction in an attempt to pur-
sue and catch the main body of Indians, on June 15 Colonel
McDermit was camped at the foot of the table mountain where
Captain Wells had been defeated in the battle of May 20, a
location "within 25 miles of the head waters of the Owyhee
River and near the boundary line of this State."

Remaining in this camp to rest the horses, establish supply
lines, and send out scouting parties to locate "the direction
taken by the hostile Indians," Colonel McDermit also dis-
patched a company of cavalry to patrol between the Humboldt and Reese rivers and ordered another to the Queens
River country to protect travelers and settlers.

He then divided his remaining force into two commands.
Retaining one hundred and fifty-seven men, a packtrain
of twenty mules, and a twelve-pound howitzer packed on
mules, he placed Captain Doughty in command of the other
unit of one hundred men and directed him to start for the
headwaters of the Humboldt River where they would join
forces at a place where "from all reports of my scouting parties
I expect to find the main body of Indians."

Colonel McDermit's orders to Captain Doughty included,
"You will scour the country between this camp and the point
above named, punishing any hostile Indians you may find.
Should you however meet any Indians whom you are satisfied
have not been connected with any of the depredations committed in this section of the country, you will afford them
every protection. You will not permit your command to com-
mit any indiscriminate slaughter of women and children."

On July 2, Colonel McDermit's command set out following
the trail of the Indians and, on the evening of the next day,
arrived in a "beautiful" valley located in Idaho Territory "at
the foot of a mountain from which the Oyhee [sic] River takes
its source." Here he found that the Indians had separated into
two parties—one traveling northwest down the Owyhee River
and the other heading east for the Humboldt River. Having

joining him in the field had a total of four hundred and seventeen men including
officers and Indian guides. The reports do not tell the number of men in the original "escort of cavalry."

previously ordered supplies sent to the head of the Humboldt, Colonel McDermit decided to follow the Indians traveling in that direction, "arriving about 30 miles above Grav [Gravelly] Ford on the Humboldt July 8th where we struck a ranch just vacated by from 50 to 100 Indians. . . . I immediately sent out 2 of our I [Indian] scouts to tell the Indians to come in, that I wanted to see them. We successed [sic] in getting 63 in camp, principally old men, women and children. Five were reported to us by our Indian scouts as having been engaged in the fight against Captain Wells and the same parties who had stolen cattle from settlers in the Humboldt country. The Chief and some 15 or 20 of his men refused to come into camp upon which I ordered 3 detachments of some 25 men each in pursuit of them . . . succeeded in killing 8 of the most desperate of the band. The Chief made his escape across the Humboldt River leaving behind him his Gun Bucher Knife Ammunition Nets [sic] and all he was possessed of. On July 12th I made a treaty with all the Indians who came to camp and were known not to have participated in any hostilities robberies etc, they promised to inform us of any further depredations that may be committed in that section and assuring us of their friendship to the whites, they pointed out and delivered up four prisoners to me who they say were guilty of depredations against the whites and this act of justice on their part convinced me of their friendly feelings to us. These four criminals I sent to Fort Churchill to be delivered to the civil authorities."

On the eighteenth of July, Colonel McDermit arrived at the "Crossing of the Little Humboldt having been informed that a party of citizens en route for Boise mines had been attacked near the Oregon line at the head of Queens River Valley. I provided my command with 40 days rations and proceeded with 120 cavalry and joined on the way by Co D 6th Cal Inf we halted at Q. R. Station within 7 miles of Oregon line. . . ."

From this location Colonel McDermit sent out three detachments to scout the country between the Queens and Owyhee rivers. Two engagements occurred in which a total of seventeen Indians were killed.

On the final page of Colonel McDermit's August 2 report (which may have been his last written communication) he wrote, "We then struck the trail of the main party of Indians who were engaged in the fight against Cap [sic] Wells o the 20th of May and whom we previously followed from th State of Nevada to Idaho Territory. We followed this trail to the point where they attacked the party of citizens en Route the Boise Mines on the 3rd of July last. From this point they have directed their course toward the white or Snow Mountains in Oregon. As soon as I rest my cavalry horses and have some shoeing done I will continue following them. I have now followed these Indians from Nev [sic] to Idaho Territory thence into Utah Territory. I then returned to Nevada and again followed them into the Oyhee [sic] in Idaho. Now I shall pursue them to Oregon."

Colonel McDermit's plan to follow the Indians into Or was not fulfilled. On August 6* his scouting party was bushed, and he was fatally wounded.

---

*The *Humboldt Register* of August 12 states that the ambush occurred on 6, and that Colonel McDermit died four hours after being wounded. Many sources say that he died on August 7.